Dialogue and Understanding
CENTRAL ASIA AND INDIA

Dialogue and Understanding

Central Asia and India

The Soviet and the Post-Soviet Era

Surendra Gopal

Maulana Abul Kalam Azad Institute of Asian Studies, Kolkata

SHIPRA

ISBN: 81-7541-237-2

First Published in India in 2005

Dialogue and Understanding : Central Asia and India

Published by :
SHIPRA PUBLICATIONS
115-A, Vikas Marg, Shakarpur,
Delhi-110092 (India)
Ph. : 91-11-55277210, 22500954
Email : info@shiprapublications.com
Website : www.shiprapublications.com

Laser Typesetting by:
R.S. Prints,
New Delhi

Printed at:
Chaudhary Offset Process
Delhi-110051

Preface

This is the first attempt to present the various facets of India-Central Asian relationship during the Soviet and the post-Soviet era in the form of a monograph. With the establishment of the Soviet regime only Indian freedom fighters were welcome in Central Asia because the Soviets tried to develop Tashkent as a base of their activities directed against British colonialism in India. This proved to be a short-lived affair as the Soviet policy makers changed their priorities and virtually debarred Indians of all hues from entering Central Asia for next three decades.

Central Asians did not forget India even in face of government indifference and loss of contact with Indians or India. Intellectuals nurtured the tradition of Indian studies as a part of their national history and as a country destined to play a significant role on world stage.

The majority of Indian studies was published in Russian language, the language of administration and higher education.

The situation somewhat changed during the Second World War when the Soviet government located several distinguished Soviet scholars on India in Tashkent in order to save them from the war raging on the Russian soil; they also used their expertise to win Indian sympathies in their struggle against Nazi Germany.

India's ties with Central Asia revived almost a decade after the Second World War ended. The changed international situation was responsible for this. Independent India and the Soviet Union, after Stalin's death came closer in order to escape and challenge the growing political and economic hegemony of the United States of America.

As Indo-Soviet relations improved after Stalin's death in 1953, the Soviet government decided to promote Indian studies in order to get inputs for its policy formulation and also to convince Indians about its genuine desire to understand their history and culture. The new upsurge in Indian studies spilled over to Central

Asia for both historical and geographical reasons. After all Soviet Republics of Central Asia were nearer to India than say Moscow or Leningrad!

During this period Tashkent emerged after Moscow and Leningrad (now Petersberg) as the third most important centre of Indian studies in Central Asia. Undoubtedly, it occupied the premier position in Central Asia in respect of Indian studies. Students from several Communist countries came here to learn Indian languages and complete their higher studies in Indian history. Tashkent's relationship with India became intimate when the government allowed admission of Indian students into local institutions of higher studies.Central Asian students joined Indian Universities and Institutes. The educational exchange was supplemented by regular visits of officials, political activists and cultural workers on both sides.

The collapse of the Soviet Union provided an opportunity both to India and the newly independent Central Asian nations to put their relationship on a new pedestal in context of the current political, economic and strategic situation.

I am responsible for the deficiencies and errors a discerning reader may find.

8 March 2005 **Surendra Gopal**

Acknowledgement

My first thanks are due to Professor Devendra Kaushik, Chairman, Maulana Abul Kalam Azad Institute of Asian Studies, Kolkata, who readily accepted my proposal and agreed to the preparation of a book on India-Central Asian relationship in the twentieth century.

I am obliged to Prof. Mahavir Singh, the Director, who allowed me extra time to complete the monograph than had been originally stipulated.

A work like this requires unstinted support from colleagues in Russia, Uzbekistan and Tajikistan. I remember them and record my gratitude to Prof. L. B. Alayev, Drs Zagorodnikova Eugenia Vanina, Azad Shamatov, Mirkasimov (the first ambassador of Uzbekistan in India), Fatih Teshbaev and Muzaffar Alimov, etc. I have a special word of thanks for Ms. Dilaram of Uzbekistan whom I occasionally consulted when in doubt about a name or an event.

Prof. Ruby Roy of The Institute of Defence Studies and Analyses, New Delhi brought for me material from Kyrgyzstan. My sincere thanks to her.

The members of the staff of Khuda Baksh Oriental Public Library, Patna, have always been helpful in providing books. I am deeply indebted to them, especially the Director Dr. Imtiaz Ahmed and his colleagues Salim Saheb, Masood Saheb and Atiq Saheb.

I thank Shipra Publications for bringing out this volume in a short span of time.

Contents

Indians in Central Asia

The First Two Decades of the Twentieth Century

Historical records disclose continuous exchange of visits by Indians and Central Asians to each other's territories at least for the last six centuries. Visitors came from a large spectrum: they included traders, scholars, artists, artisans, job-seekers, soldiers, adventurers, common men, etc.

Indians travelling to Central Asia were adherents of faiths, such as Hinduism, Buddhism, Islam, Sikhism, Jainism, Zoroastrianism, etc. They hailed from different regions of the Indian subcontinent, though it is clear that the majority of our countrymen visiting Central Asia belonged to the geographically contiguous area of the North-West, i.e. Kashmir and its adjoining areas of Ladakh, Baltistan, Chitral, etc., the Punjab, the North-West Frontier province and Sindh. Dmitriyev puts their number between six and eight thousand at the beginning of the twentieth century.[1]

The second half of the nineteenth century saw a qualitative change in the nature of Indo-Central Asian contacts. European colonial powers became entrenched in both the areas: Great Britain in India and Tsarist Russia in Central Asia. A stable monarchy in Afghanistan and fluctuating political situation in Eastern Turkistan shaped this relationship. Russia and Great Britain began to view each other's moves with suspicion; mutual fear and rivalry shaped their policies. Eventually it affected the nature of contacts between Central Asians and Indians.

Throughout the nineteenth century, British and Tsarist agents, travellers, intelligence gatherers, political analysts, in different disguises, entered each other's territories and the arena was transformed into a hot-bed of intrigues. The two European powers had started the 'Great Game'.[2]

Both, the Central Asians and the Indians were not unaware of the attitudes and conflicting ambitions of the two imperialist powers; the activities of Indian immigrants to Central Asia bears clear indication of the changed situation at the dawn of the twentieth century.

The functioning of Indian traders should now be considered in two zones: (a) in the nominally independent Khanate of Bukhara and (b) in the Russian occupied Turkistan which included the former Khanate of Kokand including the Farghana valley and the Badakshan region in the upper reaches of the Oxus river (modern Tajikistan). Afghanistan and Eastern Turkistan were the major corridors through which Indians entered Central Asia.[3]

Bukhara, the greatest distributing centre of goods in the Mawra – un – Nahar had been since the past several centuries, a major concentration point for Indian immigrants.

Growing Russian influence over the Khanate especially after the Tsar had annexed the contiguous territories covered by Samarkand, Tashkent, Ferghana valley, etc., in 1860s, added to the problems of Indian merchants.

In order to promote the interest of her mercantile community, Russia had begun dictating Bukharan Customs policies. At one point of time, Russia laid down that the duties on imported goods would be as prescribed by all- Russian Customs Union. This hurt Indian merchants who were basically importing fine Indian cotton textiles, indigo, tea, spices, etc., and paying taxes at rates less than the West Europeans. They were reduced to the position of small-time retailers.[4]

Earlier with their base in Bukhara, Indian merchants could freely travel all over the region with their goods, but now Russia started imposing restrictions. Indians were not allowed to enter the Russian-held territory without prior permission. They had to spell out the routes they expected to take while applying for permission and were not permitted to deviate from the itinerary they had outlined.

Furthermore, by the end of the nineteenth century new powerful technological forces shaping the course of trade had emerged.

With the construction of TransCaucasian and TransCaspian railways, the region had become easily accessible to industrialised nations of Europe whose steam ships carried goods to the shores of the Black Sea which were then transported all over Central Asia by the rail network. The emerging Russian bourgeoisie was keen to use the new transportation system for furthering their business; the Indians tried to counter them by boosting their exports; they began sending goods from the port of Bombay to Batumi (Poti) on the Black Sea.[5] The reduced transportation cost helped Indian merchants to bring down the prices of their goods and survive.[6] They could not, however, offset the advantages enjoyed by the merchants of industrialised nations. The inclusion of Bukhara in 1895 in the All Russian Customs Union meant a hike[7] in the taxes paid by Indians who were put to a disadvantage in comparison to their Russian colleagues. Hence in Bukhara, Indians became small traders and money-lenders. This ensured the continuity of the flow of Indian immigrants. In Bukhara only non-Muslims were permitted to adopt usury as their profession as Islamic laws banned money-lending as a profession by the Muslims.

As money-lenders, non-Muslim Indians, especially those hailing from Shikarpur in upper Sindh became a well-identified group. However, it may be noted that Shikarpuri was a common connotation for all the non-Muslim Indians especially the Hindus, who hailed from different parts of the Indian subcontinent. The Russian traveller Novitskii noted this fact towards the beginning of the twentieth century.[8]

[I]

At the turn of the twentieth century there is a likelihood that the number of Indian money-lenders increased because while the Tsarist authorities had actively adopted the policy of suppressing and driving out Indian money-lenders from territories ruled by them accusing them of exploiting the common peasant and artisan in Turkistan, the Emir in Bukhara did not discriminate against Indian money-lenders who survived there till its incorporation into Russian Turkistan in 1920.[9]

Russian authorities soon after occupying Tashkent in 1866 proclaimed a decree signed by Tsar Alexander II putting a cap on the interest rates charged by the Indians. It mandated that "all loan agreements between the Indians and indigenous population be made according to the laws of Turkestan Krai, and notarized in a colonial court, not by local *qadis*."[10]

In 1877 the Russian authorities further tightened the screws on Indian money-lenders. General Kaufman on 7 November 1877 published a new directive to 'face off the population of the region under my [Kaufman's] rule from the Indian exploitation.' Known as Circular #8560 it stated, "From this time Indians are forbidden to buy, or otherwise receive according to any contracts or penalties, land, property, even for temporary usage." [11]

Any violation was punished by deportation to Siberia. Markovits cites an instance when three Shikarpuri Hindus "had been awarded the punishment for transportation of life to Siberia for exactions in money-lending transaction." [12]

Indian merchants were hemmed with another handicap after Russian laws made the repatriation of the property of a deceased Indian to his successor an extremely complex affair.

Zagorodnikova and Shastitko have published documents which show that Russian courts because of complex legal procedures, were unable to come to a decision concerning succession even after several years.[13]

These restrictions and daunting circumstances forced foreigners including Indians to relocate themselves in the Emirate of Bukhara and avoid the Russian occupied Turkestan. [14]

Simultaneously the Russian authorities put curbs on the movement of Indian traders in Turkestan. They were barred from entering certain areas. Indian traders residing in Bukhara sent a petition to the Tsar requesting him to allow them the right of free travelling on the territory of Russian Turkistan. Their request was turned down.[15]

In pursuit of this policy Tsarist Russia imposed several restrictions on the movements of Indians in Central Asia who were barred from entering certain areas.[16]

The Khan of Bukhara, however, realised that the Indian

money-lenders performed a socially useful economic function by providing for small credit needs of the common man in his Khanate. Hence, he refrained from excluding Indian money-lenders from operating in his dominion.

Indian money-lenders continued to ply their vocation in Bukhara. This comes out very clearly from the description of Indian money-lenders in Bukhara given by the Tajik author Sadriddin Aini who had intimate personal contacts with them.

Saddridin Aini while studying in Bukhara in 1890s found out that the Hindus resided in the serai named Alimjan.[17] In three other big caravan-serais there lived more than three hundred Hindu money- lenders.[18] However, Markovits says that the serai of the Shikarpuris was known as Kanchchi serai.[19] Muslim traders from Peshawar in North-West India stayed at serai Kazi Kalan.[20]

Indians loaned small sums ranging between ten and twenty *tenegs* to the poorest section of the population, to the peasants, to the soldiers of the Khan for short periods.[21] They charged a very high percentage of interest, with the result that, only those who were extremely needy or could not get any loan elsewhere turned to them.[22]

The high rate of interest charged by the Hindus is evident from the description of Aini. The loan was advanced for either six weeks or for two months and the amount to be returned was either twice or one and a half-time of the original capital advanced.[23]

Aini also throws light on the manner in which these loan transactions took place.

The money-lender sat in his room in the *caravan-serai*. When someone borrowed, the money-lender wrote down the name of the borrower at the top of a page about fourteen inches long and two inches broad, in an Indian language along with the sum borrowed by the loanee. The transaction was never registered with the administration and these pages served as the account book for the money-lender.[24]

For the purpose of accounting, the money-lender if he had lent twenty *tenegs* for two months, wrote down thirty *tenegs* to be paid by the borrower. He then divided the thirty *tenegs* in eight equal parts in accordance with the eight weeks; the process of returning the loan commenced from the coming week.[25]

The money-lender dressed himself in a black gown which was tied round his waist by a string. He sat in his room in the *serai* till noon. He had an embroidered square cap on his head. This was the dress prescribed for the Hindu money-lender by the Khan of Bukhara so as to distinguish him from the local population.[26]

In the afternoon the money-lender went out to collect money from his borrowers. He put from forty to fifty slips in a soiled bag with the name of the borrower sticking out and walked all over the city till evening visiting different *serais,* bazaars and streets and collected money from his loanees.[27] Then he came back to the *serai.*

In the *serai,* the money-lenders generally prepared a drink from a green herb called *'Ab Sabz'* or green water. The herb was first soaked in water and was then crushed in a mortar. Thereafter it was poured through a piece of cloth and drunk. It was intoxicating, for in the aftermath there were quarrels and fights.[28]

From this account Indian readers will immediately recognize that the drink was *bhang,* a mild narcotic very popular among different sections of the population.

As Sadriddin Aini notes such a conduct created aversion for the Hindu money-lender among the local population.

The behaviour pattern of the Hindu money-lender can be seen in proper perspective if one notes the condition under which he worked.

The Khan of Bukhara had appointed a special officer *"Esaul Hindu"* to keep watch over the Hindu money-lenders.[29] This officer had under him a number of other junior officers who helped him in his work. He kept a close watch over the activities of Hindu money-lenders.[30] Through these officers the Khan of Bukhara had an exact knowledge of the property owned by each of the money-lender. The officers knew the wealth of each money-lender with such an exactitude that on the point of death he could not transfer even a penny to his other compatriots! After his death, if there was no clear-cut heir, the money was transferred to the treasury of the Khan and this was an important reason why the Emir of Bukhara did not interfere with the activities of the Hindu money-lenders, whose wealth eventually found its way to his chests ![31]

In addition to Bukhara, Hindu money-lenders were also found in other cities of the Emirate, Gizhduvan, Karshi and Babkent, etc.[32]

Hedged in with so much uncertainly, oppressed by the authorities and despised the native populace, life for the Hindu money-lender was a trauma and the evening drink of *Bhang,* helped him to forget his miseries at least temporarily.

However, there was the other section among the Indians whose members were traders and bankers and they consisted of both the Hindus (including Sikhs and Jains) and Muslims. Broadly speaking, these traders came from all over North-Western India, from Sindh (Shikarpuris), Northwest Frontier Province (Peshawaris), Punjab (Multan and Lahore) and Kashmir as well as Delhi, Bombay and Allahabad [33]

On the territory of the Bukharan Khanate Hindu money-lenders remained active till it was absorbed by the Bolshevik regime of Russia in 1920.

Hindu money-lenders also plied their profession in Badakhshan in the upper reaches of Oxus now a part of Tajikistan.

There was no clear-cut dividing line between money-lending, banking and trading. One could ply all the occupations simultaneously or concentrate on one or two of them.

The scale of operation of these traders varied considerably. Some of them were wholesalers and others were peddlers. The capital at their command showed great fluctuation; the items they traded in showed considerable variation. The description given by Sadriddin Aini again is enlightening.

Aini refers to a Hindu, Baiarji, resident in the same serai Alimjan where the Hindu money-lenders lived. He did not practise usury; he sold semi-precious stones which were purchased by jewellers and copper-smiths for beautifying objects crafted by them.[34] However, he was treated as a connoisseur of precious stones and even the Emir of Bukhara sought his advice while making purchases of jewels. Others also called upon him and sought his opinion regarding the value and quality of gems they intended to buy. He was given a certain amount for the services he rendered.[35] But what is important is the fact that he was a well-educated person and had a clear world-view.

Aini writes that he possessed a personal library which had a number of books, printed as well as in manuscript form in Indian and Tajik languages. The printed Tajik books were published in India. Baiarji could freely read and write in Tajik. Aini struck friendship with him and borrowed his Tajik books.[36] Baiarji was better dressed than his compatriots and spent his entire time reading books.[37]

When Aini expressed his anguish at the fate of Hindu money-lenders Baiarji explained to him that the British rule had brought miseries on Indians; in their homeland they were starving. Hence, they had to emigrate and earn their livelihood in foreign countries. In Bukhara Hindus had discovered money-lending to be the easiest employment. He also noted that if the Amir stopped usury by the Hindus, they would be forced to work as hired labourers. At the same time, he noted, cessation of the money-lending operations of the Hindus, will spell ruin for the ordinary poor Bukharans.[38]

Were Indian money-lenders, traders and bankers prosperous? It is a difficult question to answer. Some did reasonably well but the majority just managed to make two ends meet.

Markovits has cited some examples of prosperous Indians. Mohandas, son of Janjimal died in 1907 in the town of Kitab in the Emirate of Bukhara after a stay of thirty-eight years. The estate he left was worth 1,20,000 Bukharan *tengas*. He owned valuable land, a garden and a *serai*. [39]

Hemraj, a resident of village Kazan in the Bukharan Emirate, who passed away in 1907, owned an estate worth 67,000 *tengas*.[40]

Some Indians did build and own serais. We come across another example of a serai, owned by an Indian. From a law-suit before a Court in Russian Turkestan, we learn that a serai, owned by the late Gerimal, son of Hukumat or Hakikat Rai, was sold in 1906 in Katta Kurgan.[41]

On the territory of Russian-held Turkestan, some Indians had diversified their activities and had set up small industrial enterprises. These Indians had moved into an alternative profession after being banned from practising usury, owning cultivable land and houses on some pretext.

In face of government restrictions, Indian traders in the Russian-held Turkestan opted for cooperation with the Russian bourgeoisie. When the Russians established factories they became suppliers of raw-material. Some Indians opened their own factories. During the period 1907 to 1910 Indians owned three factories.[42] But it was clear that this could not be their main-stream activity.[43] Indians had basically turned into sellers of local handi-crafts or goods manufactured in Russian factories in the bazaars of Central Asia.[44]

The changes in the transportation system following the introduction of railways and steam-ships had enabled the Russian bourgeoie to bring their goods to Central Asia cheaply. Having consolidated its rule in Central Asia during the last three decades of the nineteenth century, the Russian state policies openly promoted the interest of the emerging Russian capitalist class. The Indian traders devoid of political support and lacking direct links with India had no option but to face decline

[II]

The opening of the Suez Canal in 1869 established direct voyages between the port of Bombay and the Russian-controlled ports on the Black Sea. The Black sea ports were linked to Central Asian markets by railways by the opening of the twentieth century. This development affected the land-based trade between India and Bukhara. It was noted in 1911 that this tendency was evident in decreasing collection of customs duties by the Russians and the Afghans.[45] Faced by the competition mounted by the emerging Russian capitalist class, Indians entered into a compromise : they also became exporters of factory-made Russian goods to Eastern Turkestan, Afghanistan and India.

In the Bukharan Khanate they combined usury with trading operations despite constraints and handicaps. Every non- Muslim, Indian paid *jiziya* or poll-tax and twice the customs duty paid by a Muslim.[46]

The situation was different in the Russian- held Turkestan.

Russia had consciously suppressed usury by Hindus and a law to this effect was promulgated as far back as 1877.[47] The government policies immediately adversely affected Indians.

Russians obstructed Indian traders in other ways also. From 1903 Indians were required to have a pass-port and Russian visa for visiting Russian Turkistan.[48] For a time Russian authorities asked the police to report on the activities of Indians as they suspected them of being spies of the Englishmen.[49]

Indian residents of Bukhara, Muhammad Sadyk and Sultan Muhammed appealed to the Tsarist authorities to lift the ban on free movement of Indian merchants in Russian-held Turkistan.[50]

The Russian government was in no mood to relent. It was trying to put as many hurdles it could to prevent Indian immigration to Russian-held Turkestan. The Russian Counsel in Bombay was specially advised in 1902 to inform the names of such persons visiting Central Asia who could be suspected of taking up money-lending after their arrival. They were to be put under police surveillance.[51] In 1908 specific instructions were issued that Indians suspected of indulging in money-lending should be denied visa.[52]

The cumulative impact of Russian policies was a sharp reduction in the number of Indians in Tashkent and also in other parts of Russian Turkestan.

The Hindu money-lenders who could not adjust to the new situation either left for the Bukharan Khanate or for Eastern Turkestan where Hindu money-lenders were permitted to ply their trade, though here again the local population looked down upon them. In fact, Eastern Turkestan became a major theatre of their activities. In 1907-08, according to a Russian officer M.S. Andreyev, there were around 200 Hindu Shikarpuris engaged in money-lending.[53] The presence of Hindu money-lenders is noted in the twenties and the thirties in Chinese Turkestan as well after they had been forced to stop commercial and usurious activities following the consolidation of the Bolshevik power in 1920 in Central Asia.[54]

[III]

Both in the Bukharan Khanate and the Russian-held Turkestan, Hindus were allowed to follow their own socio-cultural and religious norms. They were not entitled to construct a temple, but were permitted to set up their idols and icons in the *serias* where they lived.[55]

Contemporary sources indicate that the Hindus celebrated at least two of their religious festivals, *Diwali,* the festival of light and *Janmasthmi* the birth-day of Lord Krishna in full view of the public. Local dignitaries and authorities were present as their honoured guests. '*Mir Shab*', the Bukharan officer was, by custom, always invited to attend the Diwali festivities and he made it a point to be with the Indians.[56]

[IV]

In Tashkent, the administrative centre of the Russian-held Turkestan, a school for teaching Indian languages to Russian military officers was established after it had functioned for a short-while in Ashakhbad. Local Indians were recruited to teach spoken Hindustani; some teachers were also recruited in India to teach the language. A Kashmiri Kabirshah Mustafin resident in the village Bikabad in Pskentskii region of Tashkent proved to be a very popular teacher. He could teach even through the medium of Russian.[57]

Indian teachers when they went to their homeland during vacations were asked to bring in text-books when they returned. A number of books and dictionaries were published from Tashkent, which emerged as an additional centre for the development of Russian indology.[58]

It might also be noted that Indians in Turkestan began to learn the Russian language and they acted as interpreters for their compatriots before Russian authorities in the nineteenth century.

[V]

The Anglo-Russian Convention of 1907, which ushered in an era of Anglo-Russian cooperation temporarily ended visits by

Indian patriots seeking Russian-aid to overthrow the British rule, as was the case in the nineteenth century.

The outbreak of the First World War in Europe in 1914, the emergence of a pro-German regime in Afghanistan and the German support to Indian freedom fighters provided an opportunity for Indians to renew their political activities in Central Asia.

Mahendra Pratap formed a Provisional Government in Afghanistan in 1915 and sent his emissary twice to the Tsarist Governor in Tashkent in 1916. On the first occasion the Indian Mission was not entertained. Mahendra Pratap and his Foreign Minister Barkatullah took another chance and this time their emissaries were handed to the British officials who shot them dead.[59]

But things changed after the Bolsheviks came to power in Russia following the November Revolution of 1917.

The Bolshevik army intervened in order to secure the allegiance of the Emir of Bukhara. The armed conflict caused enormous loss of life and property. Indians suffered considerably. Markovits cites the application presented by K.B.Haji Karimbaksh, a rich Peshawari merchant in support of this assertion. Karimbaksh stated, "In the attack that took place at 2 o'clock at night, the invaders wrecked [sic] their vengeance on His Majesty's British subject [sic] to their hearts content. They spared neither life nor property of the British subject and duelled [sic] all the operations against Sarai Kazi Kalan which is the commercial headquarters of all the Indian, His Majesty's subjects. Incendiary bombs were dropp from Aeroplanes and the place was completely burnt to ashes." [60]

Karim Baksh was a tea merchant in Bukhara. During Balkan Wars of 1911-13, he collected donations from his compatriots for Turkey.[61]

Indians in other theatres of war suffered loss of life and property along with the local population. There was a mass migration of Indians to safer places such as Afghanistan, Iran, Sinkiang and even to homeland India. Some Indians still remained.[62]

As a group Indians were no longer a part of the Central Asian population.

The chapter of centuries-old history of Indian traders in Central Asia was over. There was no chance of reversing this trend in foreseeable near future since Bolshevik economic policies aimed at eliminating all private economic enterprise.

When peace was restored, Indians resurfaced but in a different role.

The Soviets buoyed by their success, hoped to launch a world-wide movement against colonialism, imperialism and capitalism and to put an end to exploitation of man by man.

In pursuit of this noble aim, the Soviets decided to actively support and encourage Indians, then waging a war of independence against British colonialism for the last seven decades not only on the Indian soil but also in different parts of the world. They encouraged and invited Indian freedom fighters to come to the Soviet Union and wage their war against the British rule from Moscow and also their Central Asian territories, geographically nearer to North-Western India.

Indian freedom fighters replaced Indian traders soon after their exodus, in Central Asia. A leading historian comments, "From the first half of 1919 Soviet Turkestan and in the first place its capital Tashkent became one of the leading centers for Indian revolutionaries."[63]

Some Bolshevik revolutionaries especially Weltman during their exile in Paris had been in touch with Indian revolutionaries. After the Bolsheviks became rulers of Russia, the Indian patriots knowing their aversion for capitalism, colonialism and racialism, turned to them for support in their struggle against British rule.[64]

The Bolsheviks responded positively. After the Third Communist International (Comintern) was established, the Soviet regime decided to actively promote fight against colonialism and to support freedom struggles in the colonies; a section of Indian patriots, who felt ideological affinity with the Bolsheviks aligned themselves with the new regime. Many Indians, especially those who upheld Pan Islamism were not favourably inclined towards the atheist ideology but they chose to go along with it in the hope of securing Soviet support for their ongoing struggle against British colonial rule. In December 1919, Indians in Tashkent formed the Indian Revolutionary Association.[65]

Members of this Association came from several parts of India and professed different faiths. They were united by a single desire—to win freedom for their country.

The Third Congress of Comintern was held in Moscow in 1920. It decided to use Tashkent as a base for waging war against British imperialism in the East. A group of Indian participants in the 3rd Congress at Moscow headed by M. N. Roy was sent to Tashkent.[66] They tried to recruit Indians residing in Tashkent for their cause. They formed the Indian Communist Party at Tashkent on 17 October 1920.[67] They were joined by a group of Indians headed by Acharya who had arrived from Kabul.[68] The first Indian Communist Party was formed in exile in Tashkent.

The Soviet regime needed legitimacy in the Muslim dominated Central Asia. It also needed the support of the local populace because the White Army was trying to stir up trouble. The British rulers in India knew what was cooking and were adopting counter measures. They sent Bailey to make things hot for the Bolsheviks.[69] The services of Barkatullah, an Indian revolutionary and a Pan-Islamist and a die-hard anti-British were used by the Soviets for conducting anti-British propaganda. He wrote pamphlets in Persian language; the Bolshevik government printed and extensively distributed them in Central Asia.[70]

The morale of Indians received a boost when hordes of Indian Muslims arrived in Tashkent via Afghanistan. The new Afghan King Amanullah had, who succeeded his father Habibullah after he was assassinated in 1919, facilitated their journey. The Indian Muslims had left the country with the aim of fighting against the allied powers in defence of the Caliphate. The new monarch followed 'ultra-nationalist and un-British policies'.[71]

Among the important leaders who arrived in Tashkent was Maulana Obaidullah Sirhindi, a proponent of Pan-Islamism. He left for Moscow. He was unable to reconcile himself with the atheistic principles enshrined in the Communist ideology. After staying for some months on the soviet territory, he went to Constantinople.[72]

The political activism of Indians in Tashkent was short-lived.

The Comintern fed up with their internal feuds and mutual recriminations ordered them back to Moscow; the Military School was closed in 1921 as a sequel to the Anglo-Russian agreement;[73] the students were advised to proceed to Moscow and get admitted to the newly established Communist University of the Toilers of the East.[74]

The Bolshevik regime had succeeded in consolidating itself in the Bukharan Emirate by instigating a rebellion and sending its army. The Khan of Bukhara was forced to flee. The Emirate was thereafter made a part of the Soviet Turkestan.

The British military intervention in trans-Caspia and trans-Caucasus also came to a nought; the presence of the Indian armed-forces aroused local hostility against the Indian community. On 1 May 1920 the Red Army occupied Baku and Azerbaijan became a part of the Soviet Union. Lenin described Baku as 'a Marxist window on the Moslem East'.[75]

British spies, such as Bailey, Blacker, Etherton and Macartney had sneaked into Tashkent[76] to oust 'the Bolsheviks who were described as pro-German'. The British agents were instructed to align with the anti-Bolshevik groups, and if possible, to try to bring about a rising in Tashkent similar to that they had engineered at Baku and Askhabad against the Bolsheviks by rendering financial assistance which might sound the death knell of the Bolshevik power in this region.[77] But they soon realized the futility of their efforts to overthrow the Bolsheviks and they gave up.[78] British Secret Services had failed in their mission to stir up a rising of counter-revolutionaries.

The British authorities in India, however, did not cease sending their agents to Central Asia for inciting the local population against the Bolsheviks; but even the revolt of Bachcha Saki in Kokand failed to roll back the wheel of history. Bolsheviks remained in firm control of Turkestan from the shores of the Caspian to the borders of Sinkiang.

With Bolsheviks aiming at the abolition of private control over means of production and eliminating private commerce, Indian traders and money-lenders became redundant. Some returned to India, some went to the Chinese Turkestan to which because of porus borders, access was not difficult. Private commerce and usury still prevailed in Chinese Turkestan and *Caravans* between Srinagar in Kashmir and Kashgar in Sinkiang continued to travel.[79] Usury was condemned by the locals; it was noted, "Money-lending by British subjects is not encouraged by His Majesty's Consulate-General at Kashgar-very much the contrary-money-lenders get no support from British consular officials in Turkistan".[80] Still Indians could practise usury and carry on trade.

Indians in Chinese Turkestan maintained a very fragile relationship with the Soviet Central Asia. Indian traders in Central Asia had become history.

Rest of the Indians who could neither return nor go to Sinkiang became integrated in the local population. The Census conducted in Uzbekistan in 1926 recorded all Indians as permanent residents of the U.S.S.R. and hence, it is difficult how many of them were there.[81]

[VI]

Along with scholars, travellers, traders, soldiers from India who went to Central Asia, groups of Indians belonging to the lowest rung of the social order also entered Central Asia. The Soviet indologist Oranskii discovered a group of paria in Tajikistan who spoke in a language akin to Punjabi and who with great zeal had preserved their language. Of course, they had forgotten from where their forefathers had originally arrived.[82]

In the Soviet regime the nature of Indians entering Central Asia was entirely different from the preceding centuries. In the thirties and the forties occasional visitors made their way. Only after Khruschev opened up the Soviet Union and a free India became a friend of the Bolshevik regime that Indo-Central Asia contacts were revived. Central Asia now welcomed Indian scholars, students and cultural workers instead of traders.

Footnotes

1. G.L. Dmitriyev, *Iz Istorii Sredneaziatsko-Indiiskikh Otnoshenii Vtoroi Poloviny XIX-Nachala XX V. (Indiiskiye Vykhodtsy V Srednei Azii). Avtoreferat,* Tashkent, 1965, pp.6-7. Markovits agrees with this view. He says, " The Shikarpuris were not the only merchants community from British India present in the region: there was a community of Peshawari Muslim merchants which was approximately 500-strong, and also merchants from the Punjab, Hindus, Sikhs and Muslims as well as Kashmiris (who were engaged in shawl trade) and the occasional Marwaris, Gujarati and north Indian merchants." Claude Markovits, *The Global World Of Indian Merchants 1750-1947 Traders of Sind from Bukhara to Panama,* Cambridge University Press,Cambridge (U.K.), 2000, pp.79-80
2. Devendra Kaushik, *India And Central Asia In Modern Times*, New Delhi, 1985, Chapter 5; P.M. Shastitko (chief editor), *Rossiiskiye Puteshestvenniki V Indii XIX-Nachalo XX V.*, Moscow, 1990, pp.235-244. The article deals with the visit of A.E.Snesarev to India in 1899; K.N.Warikoo, *Central Asia and Kashmir,* New Delhi, 1989, ch. 1.
3. B.I.Iskandarov, *Srednyaya Aziya I Indiya*, Dushanbe, 1993, p.91.
4. Dmitriyev, *Avtoreferat*, p.11
5. Ibid., p.9
6. Ibid.
7. Ibid.
8. B.I. Iskanderov, p.82.
9. *Avtoreferat,* p.11.
10. Scott C. Levi, *The Indian Diaspora in Central Asia and its Trade 1550-1900*, Leiden, 2002, p.251)
11. Ibid., p.253
12. Markovits, p.84 f.n. 63
13. Zagorodnikova and Shastitko (chief editors), *Russko-Indiiskiye Otnoshenya 1900-1917gg*, Moskva, 1999, (hereafter cited as *Russko-Indiiskiye Otnosheniye… 1900-1917 gg*) doc. nos. 27-34.
14. Ibid.,p.52
15. T.N.Zagorodnikova and P.M.Shatitko (Chief Editors), *Russko-Indiiskiye Otnosheniya* V 1900-1917 gg., Moscow, 1999, p.250
16. Ibid., pp.243-44
17. Sadriddin Aini, *Sobraniye Sochinenii, Vol.V (Bukhara), Moskva,1974,p.44*
18. Ibid., p.46

19. Markovits,p.104
20. Ibid.
21. Aini, p. 46.
22. Ibid.
23. Ibid.
24. Ibid., p. 44.
25. Ibid.
26. Ibid., p. 45
27. Ibid.
28. Ibid.
29. Ibid., p. 46.
30. Ibid.
31. Ibid.
32. Ibid.
33. Levi, p. 111.
34. Aini, p. 45.
35. Ibid.
36. Ibid.
37. Ibid.
38. Ibid., p. 46.
39. Markovits, p. 90
40. Ibid, p.93
41. Zagorodnikova and Shastitko, *Russko-Indiiskiye Otnoshenia 1900-1917gg*, p.50
42. G.L. Dmitriyev, "Iz Istorii Indiiskikh Kolonii V Srednei Azii" in D. A. Olderogge (chief Editor), *Strany I Narody Vostoka Indii-Strana I Narod*, Book 2, Moscow, 1972, pp. 235.
43. Ibid., pp. 238-39; *Avtoreferat*, p. 12.
44. Ibid., p. 238.
45. Iskandrov, p.93
46. *Avtoreferat*, p.13
47. Ibid., p.15.
48. Ibid.
49. Ibid.
50. Tatyana and Shashtitko, pp.244-48.
51. Ibid., p. 86 and doc. No. 61.
52. Ibid., pp. 86-90.
53. Zagorodnikova and Shastitko, p.239. Markovits has traced Shikarpuri presence in Sinkiang or Chinese Turkestan in the early decades of the twentieth century. They were, as in Central Asia, mainly engaged in providing small amounts to local poor in short-

term credit. They lived in their own *serais* and selected an elder from amongst themselves to act as their representative. He also refers to the presence of Indians from Hoshiarpur in the Punjab and Kashmir.Markovits,pp. 95-98

54. Etherton, *In The Heart Of Asia,* London, 1925, p.131. He noted, "Yangi Hissar [51 miles from Kashgar] is the happy hunting ground of Hindu money-lenders hailing from Shikarpur."
55. G.L.Dmitriyev, "Iz Istorii Indiiskikh Kolonii V Srednei Azii", pp. 239-41
56. Ibid., pp. 242-43
57. Ibid., pp. 246-47.
58. Ibid.
59. Zagorodnikova and Shastitko, pp.444-458
60. Markovits,p.104.
61. G.L.Dmitriev,*Indian* Revolutionaries *In Central Asia*, (hereafter cited as *Indian Revolutionaries...*) Gurgaon, 2002, p.26.
62. Markovits, p.105.
63. *Indian Revolutionaries...*, p.52.
64. M.P. Pavlovich ((Weltman), *India V Borbe Za Nezavisimost,* Moscow, 1925.
65. *Avtoreferat,* p.21.
66. Purabi Roy, Dutta Gupta and Vasudevan (eds), *Indo-Russian Relations 1917-1947, Part I, Calcutta 1999,* pp.38-43
67. *Avtoreferat*, p.21.
68. *Indo-Russian Relations, 1917-1947,* Part I pp. 57-59; pp.62-66, pp.66-67.
69. F.M.Bailey, *Mission To Tashkent,* London, 1946, pp.30, 55, 78.
70. Etherton, p.155.
71. *Journal of The Royal Central Asian Society*, (JRCAS), 1933, p.470.
72. During Obaidullah Sindhi's stary in Moscow in 1923, he was received four times by the Soviet Foreign Minister Chicherin. Zafar Hassan, *Ap Beeti*, (in Urdu),Lahore, 1955, pp.257.
73. Warikoo,p.118.
74. See my paper, "Comintern and the Indian Communist Party: The Early Years", *Socialist Perspective*, Vol. 28 No. 1-2, June – September, 2000, pp. 67-75.
75. *JRCAS*, 1936, p. 155.
76. T.R. Sareen, *British Intervention In Central Asia and Trans-Caucasia,* New Delhi, 1989 p. 99. Bailey in 1922 was Political Officer in Sikkim. Warikoo, p.117; P.T. Etherton, p. 124.
77. Ibid., p.101

78. Ibid., pp.104-7
79. *JRCAS,* 1933,pp.533.
80. *JRCAS,* 1933,p.486.
81. G.L.Dmitriyev, "Is Istorii Indiiskikh...", p.234.
82. I.M.Oranskii, "K Etnografii Indiyazychnoi Gruppy Parya", in *Strany I Narody Vostoka Indii—Strana I Narod*,pp.219-33

Indian Freedom-fighters in Tashkent 1917 – 1922 (Contesting Ideologies: Nationalism, Pan Islamism and Marxism)

The Russian occupation of Tashkent in 1866 ushered in a new era in politico-economic life of Central Asia. Under Russian rulers, Tashkent, the Russian administrative centre, emerged as a major trading centre for Indians along with their traditional concentration points in Central Asia Bukhara, Samarkand and Andijan, etc. Indian traders viz. Kashmiris, Peshawaris, Shikarpuris, Punjabis, etc., flocked to the city.

As Russia consolidated her hold over Central Asia, Indians grasped the essence of a new political reality; a major European colonial power capable of challenging British might in India was only one country (Afghanistan) away; its support could be sought against the British, ensconced in India. Indians disenchanted with British rule started coming to Tashkent seeking Russian support for driving out their colonial masters.[1] The tsarist rulers of Russia were happy. They saw a chance to fulfill their age-old ambition of extending influence over the Indian subcontinent;[2] Tashkent was to be the new base for Russian armies marching towards India. Indians tried to cultivate Russian support and Tashkent became a new destination for Indians keen to end British hegemony over their country.

The Russian government on its part began developing institutions in Tashkent for teaching Indian languages to their military officers. For the purpose teachers were brought from India; some of the staff was recruited from the local Indian trading community.[3] Throughout the nineteenth century the Russian army was being prepared for a possible march on India.

When the First World War began in 1914, Tashkent had a concentration of Indian traders as well as some teachers; both the groups were apolitical.

Early Efforts

As the war progressed and the British suffered setbacks, Indians were emboldened to intensify their movements against the Britishers even outside the Indian subcontinent, in Americas, in Europe, etc. Some Indian patriots established the Provisional Government of India in Kabul (the capital of Afghanistan) with Mahendra Pratap as President and Maulavi Barkatullah as Prime Minister in December 1915 with the help of Germany and Turkey, the two opponents of Great Britain.[4] From the beginning Mahendra Pratap was keen to enlist Russian support for his cause and he was able to win over the Afghan Amir Habibullah to his idea;[5] after all, the Russians were just across the Oxus river, the boundary between Afghanistan and Russian-held Central Asia. The Afghan Amir was helping Indians so as to pressurize the British authorities to enhance the monetary subsidy he was receiving from them.

The Provisional Government of India in Kabul was so excited and so sure of receiving Russian assistance that on 12 February 1916 Maulavi Barkatullah dispatched a letter to the Russian Governor General of Central Asia beseeching his support for their cause.[6] They forgot that Russia and Great Britain were allies against Germany in the war and hence, Russia would not sour her relationship with the allies by extending support to Indian freedom movement directed against British rule in India. The next day Mahendra Pratap, the President of the Provisional Government wrote a letter to the Russian Tsar Nicholas II (13 February 1916) expressing his 'dismay' at the war 'being fought between two powerful neighbours' (Russia and Germany) in Europe and expressed 'sincere hope' that 'the Imperial Highness the Tsar's (sic) will be soon able to do something in this direction' for 'the future well-being' of humanity.[7]

Indian patriots desperately wanted to enlist Russian help.

Mahendra Pratap followed this letter by another (sent through

Sardar Shamsher Singh and Mirza Mohammad Ali) on 21 February 1916 to F.V. Martson, Governor General of Russian Turkestan, seeking Russian aid for the Indian freedom struggle 'in the name of 300 million Indians' and 'in the interest of Russia and humanity'. He confessed that though they were 'obliged' to Germany and Turkey (Russia's opponents in the war) for the support extended to them, they (the Indians) remained 'neutral' in the war and they (the Indians) 'deeply respect and love Russia as their great neighbour and brother in Asia'.[8] He exhorted Russia to show 'determination' and placed his 'modest services' for bringing about an understanding between Russia on the one hand and Turkey and Germany, on the other. He requested the Governor General to send his 'golden letter' to the Tsar.

Since Russia and Great Britain were allies, the Russian Foreign Office asked its General Counsel R.A. Lisovskom to convey the news of the arrival of Indian agents from Kabul in Tashkent to the Government of India.[9]

The British Foreign Office quickly reacted and conveyed its request through its ambassador in Petrograd to the Russian authorities to arrest the Indian agents and hand them over to the British government.[10]

The Russian government, however, did not accept British request since they did not want to spoil their relations with their neighbour, the Amir of Afghanistan and therefore the decision was taken at the highest level to send the Indians back to Afghanistan.[11] The Tsar, however, asked the 'golden letter' of Mahendra Pratap to be sent to him.[12]

Before the Indian agents left, they had a meeting with the Governor General where they expressed their disappointment at their failure to achieve their objective but wanted to know if they would be permitted to go to Japan via Siberia. The Governor General did not give an affirmative reply to the later query.[13]

Raja Mahendra Pratap was not disheartened by Russia's lack of interest in his proposal. In August 1916 the Provisional Government in Kabul sent two agents with letters addressed to the diplomatic assistant to the Governor General of Russian Turkestan. It was signed by Maulvi Barkatullah.[14] The two Indians travelled on an Afghan passport and carried a diplomatic letter from the Afghan Amir to the Government of Japan. They were arrested at Termez by the Russians and information about their arrival was conveyed to the Russian Foreign Affairs Ministry.[15] The agents were Sardar Shamsher Singh[16] and Abdul Kadir Khan. The letter of the Indian Provisional Government reminded Russian authorities that they awaited the arrival of a Russian emissary from the Tsar with a reply to the earlier letter. The Indians informed the Russians that the Afghan Government had instructed the Governor of Mazar-i-Sharif to treat the Russian emissary as a state guest and ensure his safety and comfort.[17] The Russian authorities, however, placed the two Indians in Termez under strict surveillance and did not allow them to proceed further until they received instructions from their government.[18]

When Mahendra Pratap failed to receive any news from his emissaries he addressed another letter to the Governor General of Russian Turkestan on 5 October 1916. He expressed his regret that his earlier letters had not been answered; he requested a personal audience with the Tsar to convey to him certain important information about which 'he could not write' or 'could not speak to anyone'. It is not clear what news Mahendra Pratap wanted to communicate personally to the Tsar.[19]

The Russian Foreign Minister in his note to the Tsar on Mahendra Pratap's latest letter pointed out that he could not keep secret the arrival of these agents from Great Britain which had requested their arrest and their repatriation to them.[20] The Foreign Minister was unwilling to say no to Britain's request and on 22 October 1916 the two Indians were handed over to British authorities at Mashad (in Iran). The Tsar approved the decision of the Foreign Minister.[21] One of the Indians was hanged on 27 March 1917 after being found guilty in the Lahore Conspiracy Case.[22] Russia did not want to alienate its major war-time ally, Great Britain.

At this point of time Tsarist authorities in Tashkent were in no mood to listen to the request of Indian patriots; they were positively hostile.

As a perpetual optimist, Mahendra Pratap was not disheartened by the lack of response from Russian authorities. On 20 October 1916 and again on 20 November 1916 he wrote letters to the Governor General of Russian Turkestan seeking his permission to enter the Central Asian territory.[23] In the second letter he put forward the proposition that he would come to Central Asia if the government promised not to deliver him to the British authorities and was prepared to stay there as a 'prisoner of war'.[24]

At long last the Russian authorities broke their silence; they briefly wrote to him referring to his letter dated 20 November 1916. The Russian bureaucracy pointed out that in view of the close relationship between Great Britain and Russia they were unable to reply to the above-mentioned letter. They requested him to stop further correspondence.[25]

Mahendra Pratap still pinned his hopes on Russia. Mahendra Pratap thought that the change of regime after the overthrow of the Romanovs following the February Revolution of 1917 might mean a change in Russian policies.[26] In May 1917 he wrote to the Russian Military Commander for permission to travel to Central Asia. He was told that the 'change in regime did not mean any change in friendly relations between the two countries' and hence, no negotiations with him were possible. The letter also asked the local authorities to 'arrest Paratap and keep him under surveillance' if he entered the Russian territory.[27] Pratap notes, "... Kerensky's government just followed the foreign policy of the former regime."[28]

Persistent Russian refusals did not dishearten Mehendra Pratap; he remained a firm believer in using Tashkent as a base for fight against the British rulers of India. Hence, when the November Revolution of 1917 took place and the Bolsheviks came to power in Russia, he immediately turned to the new rulers and on 29 November 1917 wrote to the authorities in Tashkent.[29]

Mahendra Pratap and the Bolsheviks

Pratap began his letter by frankly showing his ignorance about the status and position of the new authorities. He briefly spoke of his earlier letters seeking permission for entry into

Russian Central Asia. He wrote about his mission, i.e. his commitment to free his country from British rule. He iterated 'he could offer some help to Russia which would also be in the interest of India and humanity'. He requested his feelings to be conveyed to the authorities in Tashkent and inform him about their response 'as early as possible'. He again pledged his services for removing misunderstanding between Russia and Germany.[30]

Little did Mahendra Pratap realize that the Bolshevik leadership had reached an understanding with the German Kaiser, who had ensured Lenin's return to Russia from exile in a sealed train. But for Lenin's arrival, we do not know what would have been the fate of the November Revolution of 1917 in Russia.

For the first time, Pratap's overture, received a positive response. Bolshevism professing faith in an ideology of anti-colonialism and anti-imperialism could not curtly turn down his request as the earlier Tsarist authorities had done. Real politik was also behind Bolshevik new policy. As Pratap noted, Russia wanted to buy Afghan grain in return for petroleum. Russia believed that he could be helpful in promoting this transaction and therefore, permitted Pratap to travel to Central Asia[31] and thereafter to proceed to Petrograd where he arrived in March 1918.[32] After three years of continuous efforts in face of repeated refusals and changes in Russian political scene and polity, Pratap was able to start a dialogue with Russian authorities on the means to be employed to attain Indian independence.

The Provisional Government of India in Kabul became the first grouping of Indian nationalists to have established contacts with the new Bolshevik government; the link of this important event was forged in Tashkent.[33] After Mahendra Pratap's journey via Tashkent to St. Petersberg Tashkent emerged as an important base for Indian revolutionaries for the next few years. Several other factors were responsible for the new role Tashkent was destined to play in Indian freedom struggle.

Indian Patriots in Tashkent

Mahendra Pratap's firm belief that Indian freedom fighters must approach Russia and his tenacity in contacting Russian authorities via Tashkent created an image of Tashkent in Indian mind as an important base for waging war against the Englishmen in India in the coming years. The Bolshevik policies as they unfolded in 1918 and thereafter guided by ideological and administrative considerations, confirmed Indians in their assessment.

The Bolsheviks had chosen Tashkent for spearheading their activities in the East and taken several measures for promoting a Communist-inspired world revolution. A powerful reason was Bolshevik anxiety to win over the support of the Muslim masses, constituting the majority of the population in the Asian region of the former Tsarist Empire. From the very beginning the Bolsheviks were conscious of the significance of the Muslim component of population not only in their country but also in the whole of the East.

They had on 7 December 1917 issued an appeal to Muslims of Russia and the East calling them to "Overthrow [the] robbers and enslavers of your country!"[34]

In order to devote their energies to this task, the new government had withdrawn from the First World War after signing an armistice on 15 December 1917. It concluded the Treaty of Brest Litovsk with Germany in March 1918.[35] After withdrawing from the War, the Bolsheviks turned their attention towards consolidating their authority among the Muslims of Central Asia. The West read Bolshevik intentions and retaliated.

An anti-Bolshevik movement, inspired by the western powers slowly emerged in Central Asia. Tashkent was in grip of turmoil in 1918; in January 1919 a failed-attempt was made to overthrow the Bolshevik authority. Thereafter the Bolsheviks grew cautious and consolidated their grip over the administration.[36]

The British authorities in India were keeping a close watch over the new situation emerging in Central Asia. As a precautionary measure in January 1918 they sent a British force under the leadership of Dunsterville[37] to trans-Caspia. British spies such as Bailey, Etherton and others went from India to Tahkent in April 1918; their mandate was to watch the unfolding of events in Tashkent and adopt suitable measures to promote British interest[38] ; they were also asked to suggest to the Indian government additional steps it should take for protecting its interest. The Soviet authorities in Tashkent aware of British policies, had taken suitable action to nullify them. One component of Bolshevik plans was to organize Indian resistance to British in Tashkent. By August 1918, the Bolshevik plan of pitting Indian freedom fighters against the British assumed shape.

Ideologically the Bolsheviks were prepared to welcome anti-imperialist and anti-colonialist support from any part of the world. They deemed it their duty 'to spread the ideas of socialism and the liberation of the oppressed nations' and 'to assemble the vanguard revolutionary forces of the East'.[39] For this purpose as early as in May 1918 when chaotic conditions still prevailed in Russia, a Federation of Foreign Communists under the Central Committee of the Russian Communist Party (Bolshevik) was organised.[40] A step forward was taken in October 1918 when an organization 'Union for the Liberation of the Peoples of the East' was set up in Moscow. Soon its unit, "The Tashkent Union" was formed.[41] The Central Bureau of Muslim Organization of the Russian Communist Party (Bolshevik) was established in December 1918 for guiding 'the Communist movement of the working people from nearby Eastern countries.' It started extensive propaganda work among migrants from Asian countries. J.V. Stalin was its chief in 1918 and early 1919.[42]

India loomed large in Bolshevik considerations even though it was an overwhelmingly Hindu-majority area; however, it had a substantial Muslim population in the tribal areas on the north-western frontier, Kashmir, the Punjab and Sindh. Russia also knew that a sizeable chunk of British army consisted of Pathans and Punjabis hailing from north-western India who professed Muslim faith. Propaganda denouncing capitalism, colonialism and imperialism among the Eastern people was a part of Soviet grand strategy to keep the British rulers in India on their toes and to prevent their interventionist forces from exerting full pressure on the Bolshevik regime.

The march of events confirmed Bolshevik fears and fully justified their policies.

The Sultan of Turkey, an ally of Germany, the Caliph of the

Muslims, had given a directive to the Muslims for conducting a *jehad* (religious wars) against the western powers.[43] As a part of the broad design to counter Western attempts to stir trouble in Central Asia, the Bolsheviks decided to use Indian card as well since Indian Muslims were unhappy with the treatment meted to the Caliph by the allied powers.

A front for conducting Indian freedom struggle was opened in Tashkent. The Indians and the Bolsheviks were now allies against the British. The Indians still kept a low profile. But the intentions of the new regime were clear. It had reversed the policies of the Tsarist and Kerensky governments; it had pledged to support in every possible manner India's fight for freedom and permitted the use of Tashkent as a base. Soon the Bolsheviks revealed their plan. Their top leader, Lenin took personal interest in this matter.

It is in this context we should appreciate the significance of Lenin receiving Khairy brothers of India, Jabbar and Sattar on 23 November 1918.[44] Next year, i.e. in May 1919, Lenin met Maulvi Barkatullah, the Prime-Minister of the Provisional Government of India in Kabul. In July 1919 an Indian delegation consisting of Mahendra Pratap, Maulvi Barkatullah, Abdur-Rabb Barq, P.B. Acharya, Dalip Singh Gill and Ibrahim, a peasant from the Punjab[45] was with Lenin.

The writing on the wall was clear. The Bolsheviks wanted 300 million Indian masses to be their allies in their worldwide struggle against colonialism, imperialism and capitalism. The Bolsheviks supported the Indian freedom struggle ideologically, politically and materially.

Bailey's mission failed; he was forced to flee. The Bolsheviks established a firm grip over Tashkent. This emboldened the Bolsheviks to step up their intervention on behalf of Indian freedom – fighters from Tashkent.

The choice of Tashkent for the purpose was well thought out. It was more conveniently accessible to Indians than any other place in the Soviet Union. At the given moment the regime in Afghanistan was hostile to the British and was allowing the Provisional Indian Government to function from its soil. It also allowed Indian patriots to keep in touch with their friends on the subcontinent. Afghanistan put no obstacle in the path of Indians who came with a desire to migrate to Central Asia.

The Coming of the *Muhajirins*

By 1919 the Soviets had informally decided to deal with the members of Indian Provisional Government of Kabul and also with members of the Indian community who were coming from Afghanistan to Central Asia.

Possibly the outbreak of the third Anglo-Afghan War in May-June 1919 influenced the Bolshevik decision to further encourage Indian revolutionaries to operate from Tashkent so as to pin British attention on the north-west frontiers of their Indian possession and divert their energies from trans-Caspian area where a British interventionist force was already creating problems for the nascent Bolshevik regime.[46]

The process was hastened by the emergence of *Khilafat* (pro-Caliph) movement in 1919 among Indian Muslims. The movement aimed at defending the power and prestige of Caliph, who after the defeat of Turkey in the First World War was forced to relinquish control over Holy Places of Islam in Mecca and Madina and was being humiliated in other ways. There was a powerful wave of sympathy for him among Indian Muslims. The '*Khilafat*' movement developed among Indian Muslims with the aim of forcing the English to restore the power and prestige of the Caliph. Muslims observed *Khilafat* days on 7 October 1919 and on 19 March 1920; a general strike was declared.[47] In August 1920, Gandhi launched the Non-Co-operation Movement, the first mass movement against British rule in India.[48] Mahatma Gandhi, the top leader of the Indian National Congress, leading the Indian anti-colonial fight forged an alliance with the pro-Caliph Muslim leaders. The Indian freedom struggle, with Muslim support, now acquired the character of India *versus* Britain.

The leaders of the *Khilafat* and the Non-Co-operation movements joined hands after a heated debate at the Allahabad Khilafat Conference on 1-2 June and the Khilafatists adopted non-co-operation as the method of political struggle.[49]

The Bolshevik calculations about India seemed to be right. They were trying to capitalize on the anti-British sentiments running high in India.

The desire of the Indian Muslims for non-co-operation with the British on grounds of religion received a boost when on 20 December 1919 Amir Amanullah, the ruler of Afghanistan lent his support to the Muslim clerics of Kabul city by his presence at a congregation where he called upon the Muslims 'to defend the faith in the wake of the occupation of Holy Places of Islam in course of the War against the Ottoman Empire and Turkey'.[50] Amanullah was a known opponent of British colonial rulers and to fortify his position, he had sent an Afghan mission under Wali Khan to Moscow on 14 June 1919. The Soviets responded by dispatching Bravin to Kabul.[51]

As the *Khilafat* movement grew in intensity, the Muslims thought of *Hijrat,* i.e. migration from India as a form of non-co-operation with the ruling British government. *Hijrat* was proclaimed by many Muslim divines for 'all Muslims except those who by their stay in India can serve their religion better and have sufficient power to fight every compulsion contrary to their religion'.[52]

Hijrat caught the imagination of the Muslim masses more than *hajj* because it had 'the additional advantage that becoming its witness or participant was much more rare and exceptional than the *hajj* and promised a much higher degree of religious deliverance'.[53]

Afghanistan became a preferred destination over Anatolia and Khanates of Central Asia because of proximity, accessibility and the anti-British stance of its ruler. Moreover, as Reetz notes, "After the Afghans almost invited the emigration and pledged to support it materially to a certain extent it was not surprising that the focus of the *hijarat* campaign primarily centred on Afghanistan."[54]

Ghulam Muhammad Aziz formed the central *Hijarat* committee on 14 May 1920 at Delhi and the *hijarat* movement was on.[55]

The exodus of *muhajirins* was a trickle in May but on 17

July a caravan of 846 *muhajirins* entered into Afghanistan. [56] A special train from Sindh was chartered by the Larkana chief Jan Mahammad Junejo and it passed through the provinces of Sindh, the Punjab and NWFP. It created unprecedented enthusiasm among the local population.[57] The British government was now worried.[58] because the tribal population had been aroused and could create problems for the British.

On its part, the Afghan government opened a reception centre for the *Muhajirins* at Jabal-us-seraf (seraj), a village forty miles from Kabul.[59] The estimated number of *muhajirins* arriving in Kabul was between 18,000 and 50,000.[60] The sudden immigration of so many Indians placed a heavy financial burden on the Afghan government who were unable to meet the expenses of *muhajirins*; the lower-rung Afghan officials in order to discourage the flow of Indians now put a number of hurdles and harassed the *muhajirins* in a variety of ways.[61] The *muhajirins* were compelled to leave Afghanistan. It was reported that 3,000 *muhajirins* had returned to India via the Khaiber pass.[62]

Another section of the *muhajirins* quit Afghanistan who instead of coming back to India, they proceeded towards the Soviet Central Asia. They were passionately attached to the cause of the Caliph and ouster of the British from India. Some of these *muhajirins* provided a nucleus for creating a well-motivated and cohesive group of Tashkent-based freedom fighters, who put their heart and soul into the impending struggle against the British rule.

Shaukat Usmani, one of the *muhajirins* has thrown light on the reasons forcing them to decide on this course of action.

After entering Afghanistan they met General Nadir Khan, the Afghan War Minister and sought arms 'to fight the British on the North-West frontier area.'[63] General Nadir Khan expressed his inability to meet their demands. These Indian *muhajirins,* Akbar Khan Qureshi, Mian Akbar Shah Khattak, Gauhar Rehman, Abdul Majid, Sultan Khan, Rafiq Ahmad, Fazl Ilahi Qurban, Ferozuddin Manswi, then decided to proceed to the Bolshevik-controlled Central Asia to procure arms; for the moment they did not disclose their plans to the Afghan officials as they were apprehensive of their opposition.[64] Their fears were well-founded.

The Afghan bureaucracy refused them permission to cross over into the Bolshevik-held territory; the *muhajirins* (eighty-two in number) defied their orders; they trekked to the borders of the Bolshevik Central Asia where they reached in August, 1920[65] after suffering great hardships and deprivations. Luckily, the Bolshevik authorities at Termez, during their first stop in Uzbekistan, welcomed them enthusiastically; the civil population also received them cordially.[66] They were deeply touched by the hand of friendship extended to them; they now had a strong feeling that Bolshevik help would be forthcoming in their fight against British colonialism.

The Soviet authorities were sympathetic and sensitive to the desires of the *muhajirins* since they could be easily motivated to fight against the British. However the *muhajirins* were not a homogenous lot: some of them were intensely religious; the atheist ideology of the Bolsheviks was anathema to them; they were keen to proceed to Bukhara and thereafter to Turkey to defend the Caliph against the invading forces. A section, however, was politically alive and was keen to drive out the British from India. They decided to stay with the Bolsheviks and to try to understand their ideology and to observe the socio-economic transformation going on under the new regime. They hoped to fight for India's independence with active moral and material support of the Bolsheviks.[67] The Bolsheviks welcomed their decision because *muhajirin* support would raise their prestige in the eyes of the Muslim population of Central Asia.

The Bolsheviks also tried to dissuade the first group from leaving their territory; they pointed out the disturbed conditions on account of the roving lawless Turkoman horse-men on the road. They had become a law unto themselves as the local administration had collapsed because a civil war was raging in the country. Eventually, both groups agreed to work together and proceeded towards Kerki on boats provisioned by the Bolsheviks. In course of the journey they were arrested by the troops of the Bukharan Amir.[68] Death stared in their faces but fate intervened; they remained safe and rejoined the Bolsheviks.[69]

The *muhajirins* discovered a safe haven in Soviet Central Asia.[70] The *muhajirins* in Afghanistan with the tacit support of Afghan authorities who considered them a burden on their economy, continued to pour in Uzbekistan; they swelled the number of Indian immigrants in Tashkent during the rest of 1920 and the following years. With the advent of *muhajirins* in Tashkent, a new chapter in Indian freedom struggle began.

Reetz on the basis of Frontier Intelligence Diary maintained by the British authorities has a different explanation for the increased flow of *muhajirins* to Soviet Central Asia.

According to the Frontier Intelligence Diary, Suritz, the head of the Bolshevik Mission in Afghanistan, persuaded some of them to go to Tashkent where Bolsheviks would train them in the use of modern weaponry. The Bolsheviks wanted to use these immigrants for their political purposes.[71]

Whatever be the motivating factor, *mujahirins* continued to enter the Soviet territory with or without the approval of the Afghan government.

The *mujahirin* factor explains the presence of more Muslims than Hindus among Indians during this period in Tashkent. The Bolsheviks extended all support to Indians in carrying out their fight against the British. They could act in favour of Indians because a number of favorable circumstances had emerged.

In the first quarter of 1920, the Bolsheviks were in full control over the situation in Uzbekistan. They had suppressed the Basmachi rebellion. With the surrender of Basmachi leader Madamin on 6 March 1920, the movement had lost its force.[72] In August 1920, a revolutionary outbreak in Charjui supported by the Red Army saw the fall of the Amir of Bukhara.[73] The Second Congress of Comintern held in Moscow in July 1920 had decided to support and promote all anti-colonial movements; the expulsion of the British from India was high on their agenda since India was the largest colony in the world.

Lenin's formulation 'about the need for Communists to enter into temporary alliances with bourgeois democracy of colonies and semi-colonies without losing their own political independence in the process' became the core of Soviet policies at this Congress.[74] M.N.Roy (an Indian), who had been invited for the Congress from Mexico was now put in charge of the Eastern Section of the Comintern; he imparted a new vigour to this task.

Lenin's support to Indian revolutionaries in the Second

Congress of the Comintern was not accidental. In May 1920 he had sent a congratulatory message to Abdur Rabb Barq, Chairman of Indian Revolutionary Association in Kabul which had passed a resolution at its meeting on 4 March 1920 supporting the Bolshevik regime.[75]

The Second Congress of Comintern had set up a small subcommittee of five members called "Small Bureau" which was 'to be in permanent session as the supreme policy-making as well as executive organ of the International'.[76] Roy was coopted as its member.[77] "It passed two resolutions (1) To hold the First Congress of the Oppressed Peoples of the East at Baku; and (2) To set up a Central Asiatic Bureau of the Communist International at Tashkent."[78]

Comintern's policy with respect to Indian freedom struggle was to be implemented under the guidance of M. N. Roy and Tashkent was selected as his headquarters.

Roy did not attend the Baku Congress held in September 1920 attended by 1891 delegates out of which fourteen were Indians.[79]

Zinoviev, President of the Comintern, presided over the Congress. He stated that the Soviets were prepared to support any revolutionary fight against the British Government. While referring to India he spoke of the Amritsar massacre and the consequent terror in the Punjab as an illustration of the methods which "the civilized English imperialists" were using 'to restore order' in the East.

At the same Congress, the Bolshevik theoretician Karl Radek proclaimed Britain to be 'the principal villain'.[80]

The Congress gave the call, 'Arise like one man for the Holy War against the British conqueror.' It exhorted, 'Arise, all of you, for the fight against the common enemy, for fight against imperialistic Great Britain.'[81]

Tashkent as a Centre for Indian Revolutionaries

The Indian participants at the Baku Congress were vocal in denouncing imperialism; they demanded full support for their struggle against their British masters of India. Indian delegates assured the Comintern that feelings against British imperialism were running high in the country. They expressed the hope that with Comintern support it might become a movement and be a great embarrassment to British colonialism. Comintern chose Tashkent to be the base from where the battle was to be conducted. Comintern had committed itself to support anti-British struggle of Indians. Roy, Sokolnikov and Safarov constituted the Central Asiatic Bureau of the Comintern.[82] Roy had the great opportunity to mobilise *Tashkent Indians*, who, in fact, were waiting for proper leadership.

The decision of the Comintern to set up the Central Asiatic Bureau of the Communist International at Tashkent thrust the lime-light on Tashkent as an important centre for waging war against colonialism. On the Euro-Asian continent there were now three major concentration points of Indian revolutionaries Berlin, Moscow and Tashkent. The last was geographically nearest to India and had the largest number of Indian revolutionaries. Their number was continuously increasing because of newer arrivals. But as stated earlier, they were an amorphous lot, driven by conflicting aspirations.

The character of Indians residing in Tashkent had changed; traders were trying hard to leave not only the city but the country since private trade and moneylending in which they had specialised had been totally banned. Some had emigrated to the neighbouring Chinese Turkestan, where private business and moneylending were legal activities. The trader-cum-moneylender segment no longer existed among Tahkent Indians. The new Indians arriving in Tashkent were revolutionaries. They had established their base in Tashkent attracted by the promised Soviet support. They were determined to try their best to oust the British rulers of their country. During the next few years, they made efforts to achieve this goal.

The number of Indians in Tashkent kept on increasing ;Tashkent attracted Indian deserters from British Army stationed in Persia. Some of the new arrivals had left the British army to carry on fight against British colonialism; many of them had no clear-cut motivation.

Some of the old Indians still left in Tashkent were trying to get out of the country with their assets to either Sinkiang or Afghanistan or Persia and were not interested in the Indian freedom struggle.

However, some of the *muhajirins* arriving in Central Asia were totally committed to driving out the Britishers. They swelled the ranks of Indian revolutionaries. A section of the *muhajirins* was keen to proceed to Turkey to fight the invaders. It had no interest in Indian freedom struggle.

The Indians of Tashkent remained a mixed crowd. This is evident from the fact that the first Red Congress held in Samarkand in February 1920 was attended by 'delegates from Pamir, Afghanistan, and the Himalayan races' and '[delegates] from other cities of Inner India and even Ceylon'.[83] In December 1920 it was claimed that, "During the last nine months of 1920 the Propaganda School turned out 3500 trained instructors, including 930 Hindus... Chief attention was paid to the representatives of the Indian races, and only fully converted Socialists were sent to India. The Propaganda School is [not] confined to Turkestan, but has branches throughout Southern Asia... The most valuable classes are those recently established in Delhi and Benares, which are working splendidly under the eye of Englishmen. A report on the Delhi organization states that it was founded on July 6 last, and by November contained 91,000 active members paying subscriptions. 120,000 sterling had been collected, and the regular monthly subscriptions amounted to 15,000."[84]

It is difficult to verify the facts adduced above but as Samra points out, "... the Bolshevik policy at the time was to put pressure on Great Britain for the resumption of diplomatic relations, and this policy was made easier by the revolutionary ferment in India and the Middle East."[85] May be the Soviets touted exaggerated Indian response to Soviet propaganda to impress the British regarding the Soviet potential to stir up trouble in British colonies.

Support to Indian revolutionary movement with its base at Tashkent was used as a tool to check British intransigence, to promote the wider interests of the Soviet state and also to extend a helping hand to the Indian freedom struggle. The Soviets did not neglect their state interests.

1920 was the year when the Soviet state had launched "operation recognition" and on 31 May 1920 its representative Leonid Krassin called upon the British Prime Minister Lloyd George and President of the Board of Trade Sir Robert Horne to conclude a trade agreement between the two countries. [86]

M. N. Roy left for Tashkent after the Second Comintern Congress ended in Moscow to guide Tashkent Indians. He was to organise Indian revolutionaries and direct their activities against their British rulers. Since M. N. Roy's prestige as a capable organiser was very high in the Comintern, he was entrusted with this highly sensitive and important task. Earlier a proposal for sending him as a Soviet envoy to Kabul had been turned down because the Afghan government thought it might annoy the Britishers.[87] Instead, Raskolnikov, a confirmed Bolshevik was sent, who before leaving for Kabul asked M. N. Roy to arrange for the supply of arms to tribals on the north-western frontier of India, so that the British rule in India could be weakened and the Khilaftists got a chance to overthrow it.[88]

Roy in Tashkent

M. N. Roy arrived in Tashkent with two train-loads of arms and ammunitions and a full-fledged staff to open a military training school so as to create and equip a liberation army for India.[89] The Bolshevik government and the Comintern were seriously pursuing the idea of helping Indian patriots to oust their British masters.

Roy found that Tashkent Indians (old residents) who were basically traders were keen to get out of the country and for this purpose sought Roy's good offices and assistance.[90] When Roy asked them to make anti-imperialist propaganda among British Indian troops, they showed no enthusiasm.[91]

Similar was the attitude of Indian traders in Bukhara who 'did not believe in the possibility of liberating India'. They thought once the Russian influence from Bukhara was eliminated, trade between India and Bukhara could be resumed 'under the protection of the British Indian army in Khorasan.'[92] Roy could not get recruits from old Indian residents in Tashkent and Bukhara.

Undaunted, then Roy turned his attention to another group of Indians – the deserters from British army stationed in Persia. These deserters were mostly Muslims (Pathans from north-western frontier of India) and were eagerly trying to go to Turkey to fight for the Khilafat.[93] Roy persuaded them to stay back and from amongst them proposed formation of detachments of an irregular force which as an auxiliary to the Red Army, would patrol the trans-Caspian railway from Krasnovodsk to Merv 'as a preparatory exercise to a major offensive to drive the British invaders back'.[94]

These 'deserters', Persian revolutionaries and Russian Communists were trained in the use of 'superior arms' machine-guns, artillery, etc., and Roy claims that it was the 'first International Brigade of the Red Army' and it 'participated in several engagements with the British Indian troops on the Meshed-Askabad road' and forced the enemy to abandon 'their outposts along the Persian frontier.'[95] Some of the able 'deserters of British Indian army' rose to high position and were subsequently promoted to the rank of officers.[96]

Roy noted that the news of 'deserters' becoming officers travelled to the British Indian troops and the rate of desertions increased and the 'International Brigade soon became an effective auxiliary of the Red Army'. It ensured the safety of the 'Kransnovodsk-Merv railway' which helped the transport of petrol from the Caucasus.[97]

A little later Roy thought that *muhajirins* arriving in Tashkent from India via Afghanistan could also be recruited to the army. When he heard the news that a group of Indian *muhajirins* trying to sneak into the Soviet Union from Afghanistan via the Pamirs had been arrested by the Bukharan authorities and were being tortured, he persuaded the Red Army to rescue them, a task which was easily carried out.

The freed *muhajirins* numbered 'some seventy odd men:[98] around fifty of them came to Tashkent and the rest insisted on proceeding to Turkey to participate in *jehad.* [99] Some of them were given political education, though a section was opposed to it.[100] These had left India to fight for the Caliphate.

Formation of the Indian Communist Party

At this point the Soviets took into confidence a contingent of Indians from Kabul consisting of Abdur Rab and Acharya. These Indians already styled themselves as Communists.[101] Politically motivated, the Indians insisted on the formation of the Communist Party. The Communist Party born in these circumstances had Muhammad Shafiq who had arrived with Acharya, as Secretary.[102]

At the inaugural meeting held on 17 October 1920 seven members were present including Mrs Evelyn Roy and Mrs Abani Mukharjee.[103]

The formation of the Communist Party of India in Tashkent helped Roy to intensify political activities. Personality clashes almost immediately began between Roy and Rabb and Acharya. However, the nascent Communist Party seriously took up political work among the Indian Community. At a meeting of the Party held on 18 December 1920 the 3-men Central Committee (Acharya as Chairman, Shafiq as Secretary and Roy as member)[104] was asked to 'take steps to have Communist propaganda made among the non-English speaking Indians in Tashkent'.[105] The Indian Communist Party without any delay set about its work.

On the same day, the Committee also decided 'to organise a translation staff in order to provide work for the printing presses'. The Soviets were keen that extensive propaganda work about the achievements, policies and ideology of the Soviet state should be carried out among immigrant Indians. But internal contradictions among Indian leadership came to the fore almost immediately. This was fuelled over the question of the status of Acharya.

The Committee discussed the question whether Acharya, now a member of the Indian Communist Party could retain his membership of the Indian Revolutionary Association. Acharya signified his willingness to resign from the Indian Revolutionary Association but pointed out it might create bad blood between the two organisations. He was then 'deputed by the Party to work with the I.R.A. for the furtherance of good relations & a spirit of cooperation on the part of the later, but that henceforth C. Acharya should consider himself not as a member of the I. R. A. but as a member of the I. C. P. deputed to work within that organisation.'[106] About the propaganda work, the Committee was informed that members gave lectures to students of Military School; plans were afoot to open 'classes for trade – unionism for Indians' in the Tashkent Trade Union Section.[107]

The question of dual membership remained a point of contention. It started a power struggle between Acharya and Rabb, both representing the Indian Revolutionary Association and M. N. Roy. The matter could never be sorted out to the full satisfaction of all. Eventually, it resulted in the eclipse of the Indian Revolutionary Party. The relations between the members were soured. It had adverse consequences for the newly-established Indian Communist Party and the Miliary School in Tashkent.[108] Despite factional quarrels among Indian patriots, Tashkent, was now a centre for guiding political and revolutionary activities in India.

Activities of the Indian Communist Party

We earn of the activities of Indians from some of the communications sent by the members of the newly-formed Indian Communist Party (ICP) in Tashkent after they had drafted a programme for the constitution of a Provisional Revolutionary Committee in November 1920. The Programme was published in *Izvestia (*Tashkent) on 1 December 1920.[109] It was extremely ambitious. The Provisional Revolutionary Committee wanted to emerge as the supreme policy-making body for Indian patriots all over the world fighting against British colonialism. This is the impression from a letter written by Abani Mukharjee.

On 30 December 1920 Abani Mukharjee a founder-member of ICP sent a long letter to Shiva Prasad Gupta, a revered Congress leader in Benares wherein he justified the formation of a Provisional All-India Central Revolutionary Committee as a 'supreme body for directing the Indian Revolution'. He justified this by pointing out the problems faced in 1915 by the Kabul-based Indian Provisional Government. According to him the Provisional Government in Kabul was in no position to coordinate the activities of Indian patriots active in different countries of the world such as Turkey, Germany, USA, etc. He exhorted him to attend the meeting of the Congress to be held in Kabul or Tashkent during the coming summer. He specially sought the presence of Bhai Parmanand, Sanyal brothers and Damodar Swarup Seth in the coming Congress. He, however, clarified, '... we want revolutionaries and not constitutionalists...'[110]

Abani outlined his ideology of communism as '...our aim is to establish universal peace and happiness by destroying Classes, Private Property and the wage-system as it exists under Capitalism.'[111]

Criticising Gandhian politics of conciliation between labour and capital, he asserted, '...instead of doing the real revolutionary work, the Indian leaders are spending their time and energy for non-essential non-cooperation movements. Remember that countries can never be free without bloodshed; if you have the idea of doing it without blood, then better go to Himalaya and don't disturb us.'[112]

The Tashkent-based Indians from the very beginning directed their attack against Gandhian ideology, now dominating the Indian National Congress. Sitting far away from India, these patriots were unable to gauge the influence Gandhi had acquired over the Indian masses. They continued to emphasise their policy initiatives.

M.N. Roy and Abani addressed another letter to Gandhiji on 3 January 1921,[113] wherein they invited him to attend the coming meeting of All India Revolutionary Congress which would 'elect a truly representative Central Revolutionary Committee and frame an all-India Revolutionary Program and plan of work, and create from all groups and organisations one central Revolutionary Party for carrying on the work and which will receive, through the Central Committee, the help which is available here.'

Another letter conveying invitation for attending the proposed Congress was dispatched to Abdul Gaffar, President, The Liberation League, Kabul on 6 January 1921.[114] Besides, inviting him to the proposed Congress, it referred to the visit of two revolutionaries from Kabul, Haq and Iqbal, who were briefed by the Committee about its programme and who were instructed to advise about it to Gaffar on their return to Kabul. It also referred to the obstructive attitude of the Afghan government in matters of transporting arms to the tribal areas bordering India.[115]

The Committee also appointed Mohammad Ali as its accredited representative to Kabul.

Tashkent was the base from where attempts were being made to direct India revolutionary activities in Kabul; Kabul was accorded importance because Indian revolutionaries wanted to penetrate into British India through Kabul.

Another letter to Maulavi Abdul Karim, on 7 January 1921 in Charmkind (in tribal area) detailed the problems faced by the Committee in sending arms owing to the refusal of the Afghan government to permit their transportation through their territory. It expressly referred to the refusal of the Afghan ambassador Abdul Hadi Khan to allow transportation of arms. It said, "The Indian revolutionaries are not even allowed by the Afghans to carry money from here."[116] In order to overcome the Afghan reluctance to support Indian efforts, it exhorted Maulavi Karim and other Indian revolutionaries 'to exert your influence upon the Afghan government in order to make it change its present policy and permit us freedom to work within its territory.'[117]

The Committee also thought it worthwhile to address a letter to Raja Mahendra Pratap, Head of the Provisional Government and Maulana Barkatullah, the Prime Minister on 7 January 1921.[118] The objective of the letter was two-fold: first, to extend support to Mehmet Ali (Mohammad Ali), the accredited representative of the Tashkent Committee in Kabul and secondly, to urge upon them to 'find a way of making the Afghan Government change its present attitude towards the Indian Revolutionary Movement.'[119]

Thus the entire effort was directed at transforming Tashkent into the premier concentration point of Indian revolutionaries in the world with the support of the Comintern. Simultaneously they were trying to develop Afghanistan as a safe conduit for supplying arms to revolutionaries in India.

The Indian Revolutionaries tried to contact their compatriots in the Emirate of Bukhara (mainly in Bukhara), in Afghanistan and in Andijan in the Ferghana valley from Tashkent.

Andijan had a thriving Indian trading community even in

pre-Revolutionary days and it was reasonable to carry the new message of Indian liberation struggle to them because they could from a link with Indians residing in the Chinese Sinkiang owing to geographical proximity. Furthermore, this was an alternative route to India which skirted Afghanistan and could, if need be, used to transport men, materials of war or publicity to India.

The immediate reason for Indian revolutionaries to turn to Andijan was the presence of Kashgar revolutionaries, who had been forced to quit their country because of the oppression of local authorities. The Soviets were keen to support them and one of their officers Raskolnikov was already there. Acharya had also reached there. [120]

Roy also sent Shaukat Usmani to Andijan to help Acharya but the latter left immediately; Usmani stayed back and was put 'in charge of the arms'.[121]

Most of the Indian merchants in Andijan wanted to know how they could help the revolutionaries. Usmani suggested that the young should go to Tashkent and receive some political training. Some of them did come to Tashkent and joined the Military School.[122] But the older among them were skeptical and were still inclined to support the Britishers.

Besides this major activity, the Indian Communist Party also conducted classes for political education of the Indian immigrants and also opened a Military School to impart training to them in the use of sophisticated arms.

Educational Work

First, they started three-week courses on history, economics, working-class movement and socialism for the Indian immigrants. However, they were not very successful as very few among them were educated. Mostly, they were just literate and could not appreciate the necessity of broadening their political vision by studying social-sciences.[123] As soon the leadership realised the futility of these classes, they changed their methods. Instead they started to arrange weekly lectures and talks for the Indian immigrants which mostly covered current topics and the current situation in India, the importance of the Russian Revolution and revolutionary developments around the world.[124] The Committee was happy that weekly lectures were liked by the immigrants and it noted, '... and it is gratifying to find a steadily – growing tendency towards political rather than religious ideology in their outlook.'[125] They were able to conduct a two-week debate on the draft-programme they had drawn for the Indian revolution.[126]

Persists notes, "Tashkent schools and various courses played a certain role in the political education of the Indian revolutionaries. Several immigrants went to primary school to learn to read and write in Russian; 15 attended the Tashkent Party School for Muslims, and some Indians were among the students of the Turkestan Trade Union School."[127]

The Soviets aware of strong anti-Communist propaganda among the Muslims had opened a special School to educate the believers.

Besides, ensuring political education for immigrant Indians, the Communist Party also brought out a significant amount of publicity material on Communism, Comintern and the situation in the Soviet Union. These were to be sent to India. The following works were published in English and Urdu[128] : *A Manifesto of Turkestan Bureau of the Comintern* (10,000 copies), K. Marx's Preface to the *Communist Manifesto* (4,000), *Draft theses on the Eastern Question for the third Congress of the Comintern (*250,000 copies) probably by M. N. Roy, etc. All these were published in a short span of six weeks from May to 16 June 1921. During this period they also prepared for publication an appeal to the Indian youth, an appeal to Indian soldiers in Iran and some other items for publication in Urdu and English. Undoubtedly, the Indian revolutionaries were unsparing in their efforts to change the fate of their motherland.

The Indians also brought out a bilingual paper *Zamindar* in Urdu and Persian with Mohammad Sahfiq as editor. The objectives of the paper were:

To unite all revolutionary groups in the east: To expose the cruelties practised by the British in India: To prepare the Indian working class for revolutionary action: To expose the slanderous campaign of the British press against Communism and Soviet Russia.[129]

We do not know how many issues were published. But it underlined the feeling that wider publicity to the aims and objectives of ICP must be given in order to win over masses in India.

When it was realized that sending publicity material from Tashkent to India was a herculean task, a decision was taken to establish a printing press on the north-western borders of India and Akbar Khan Qureshi was entrusted with this task. He managed to send printing machines to the tribal areas but before something concrete could be done, he was arrested.

Akbar Khan was, in fact, sent to express Comintern's solidarity with the Indian National Congress and the Khilafat, but as we know he fell into the hands of the British Police.[130]

Tashkent Military School

The Tashkent Military School appeared to have held greater attraction for Indian immigrants. Obviously, the *mujahirins,* who had left India to fight for the Caliphate thought that a spell at the Military School would equip them much better for the task ahead.

The formation of the Military School was announced in an Order of the Day issued by the Turkestan front on 11 October 1920. It said that the All-India Central Revolutionary Committee had set up the first Indian Commanding Course for All Arms. N. A. Keselev was put in Command. The School was also known as "Indusky Kurs". It was allotted a shooting range off the Chirchik high-way near Tashkent.[131]

The School was opened with great pomp; Russians stayed away because Anglo-Russian Trade negotiation were going on and the Soviets did not want to jeopardise it. But Britain was certainly alarmed.[132]

Some of the educated Indians excelled at gunnery; some learnt flying, then still in infancy and subsequently made their mark as aviators in the Red Army.[133] However, when the British lodged a strong protest, the Military School was disbanded and the inmates were sent to Moscow where they joined the University of the Toilers of the East.

There were frequent changes at the top and even the staff

was a conglomeration of people of different nationalities, Slovene, German, Byelorussian, Tatar, etc. [134]

The School lasted for only seven months. It closed down on 27 April 1921.[135] It had started with ten students on 1st November 1920 and at the time of its closure, it had thirty-five students on roll.[136]

The first group was enrolled in the air-department, functioning under Flight Commander V. V. Goppe. When the second group joined, an infantry-machine-gun section was opened.[137]

But The School could never get going; it suffered from a chronic shortage of teaching staff. Above all, the students barring a few were full of Pan-Islamic idealism and John the Commandant of the school remarked, "we are going to train not an army of revolution, but an army of God."[138]

When the School was disbanded, some of the students were shifted to other military academies as per their qualifications; some opted for the Toilers of the East University in Moscow.

Even though the Military School functioned for a short period it won praise from its students. Shaukat Usmani writes, "though the number of the Military school students was not very large, yet the training was praiseworthy."[139]

It must also be noted that in the aftermonth of the Bolshevik Revolution of November 1917, the British had realized that the Bolsheviks were pursuing their ideology of world revolution and might develop Tashkent as a base for extending support to Indian freedom fighters in Central Asia, in Afghanistan and in Chinese Turkestan. Hence, Bailey was sent to report on the situation there. Simultaneously, a number of spies were also recruited, some from among the Indian residents and some in India. British spies from India were sent from 1920 onwards in the guise of *muhajirins.* They were to report on the activities of Indian patriots to British colonial authorities.[140]

Zakaria or Rahmat Ali of Lahore had reached Tashkent in February/March 1919 via Bukhara after escaping from a prison in Afghanistan. Here Bravin who was to leave for Afghanistan as representative of the Soviet Foreign Office, picked him up. Bravin was attracted to Zakaria because of his fine knowledge of

Persian and English and familiarity with the Afghans as he had spent three years in prison there. Bravin took him to Kabul. In Kabul Zakaria earned reputation as a Bolshevik and was elected to the Executive Committee of the Provisional Government. In October 1920 he was sent to Russia to study Marxism. In October 1921 he went to Bukhara for some organizational work. He was trusted by Comintern and was in 1922 sent to Persia. He translated *Communist Manifesto* of Karl Marx into Urdu.[141]

M. N. Roy was conscious of this situation that all his moves would be reported to the British authority.[142] He noted, '... even Tashkent was full of enemy spies in those days. They could take advantage of the disaffection of the Indian emigrants, and with a little money purchase their services. Before long, it was discovered that the apprehension was not unfounded, and I was placed in the delicate situation of dealing with suspected enemy agents as they were dealt with in those days in Russia."[143]

Roy recounts one particular incident when the arrival of an important person from India was reported to him. He was also told that the person was keen to meet him. On talking to him Roy became unsure of his credentials as he says, "Because of the fact that Turkestan was then the hot-bed of enemy espionage,..."[144] He reported the matter to the local Cheka chief whose investigations showed that the person 'spent all his days until late in the bazar', and mixed with 'Indian traders who were suspected of British espionage.' [145] Two members of Indian Provisional Government in Kabul who happened to come to Tashkent confirmed him 'as a British Agent'.[146] He was ultimately put to death by the Soviet authorities. [147] I have not been able to discover his identity.

No wonder many of the Indians who returned from Tashkent to India in 1921 were arrested on the basis of prior information received by the British authorities on their activities and the British government instituted the "Moscow-Tashkent conspiracy Case."[148]

If the dawn of the year 1921 promised new vistas for Indian revolutionaries in Tashkent it also opened up a period of mutual recrimination and personality clashes among them.

Factional Feuds in the Indian Communist Party

The Indian Communist Party split up in two factions: the Moscow faction headed by Roy and Abani Mukharjee and the Kabul faction led by Acharya and Abdur Rabb (Peshaware) Barq.

Shaukat Usmani has described the effects of the internecine quarrel between the two factions. "Circumstances forced us to forget for the Time being our military ambitions. Our very individuality was lost in the whirlpool of the factional fight of others, and we veritably became the fuel. The big theoreticians drowned us in their arguments about building a theoretical background for the Indian Revolution."[149]

Shaukat Usmani further wrote, "…so I, together with some lettered comrades were in a tricky situation. We did not know whom to join."[150]

Almost from the time the Indian Communist Party was formed, tension between the two groups was obvious to any discerning observer.

The reasons for this factional feud were many. The background of both Roy and Abdur Rabb Barq (and his colleagues) was different. Barq at Kabul had been actively propagating the cause of Independence and this was for him the prime objective. For Roy steeped in Marxist principles a bourgeois revolution was a counter-revolution and hence, an anathema. For Barq independence was the dearest value. Even while accepting communism he insisted that the association "shall defend the principles of Communism" and "make nationalistic and religious propaganda."[151]

Roy with his performance at the Second Congress of Comintern and nearness to Lenin believed that the triumph of the proletarian revolution should be his primary objective. Inability to secure Afghan permission for sending arms to India did not dim his ardour for precipitating a mass armed upsurge in India. He condemned both religiosity and nationalism. The only common bond between the two factions was the hatred for British colonialism but this was not enough to ensure unanimity about their objective and the method to achieve this or the formulation of a long-tern strategy for this purpose. It was therefore, not unusual that even after the formation of the Indian Communist Party, Rabb and Acharya tried to preserve the identity of Indian Revolutionary Association to which they originally belonged.

Roy was sent from Moscow to achieve: "first the convocation of an all-India Congress of revolutionaries and the establishment of an all-India revolutionary centre capable of preparing and holding, in particular, this Congress, second the immediate launching of the military and political training of revolutionary forces."[152] Roy concentrated his attention on performing these tasks.

When forming the all India Revolutionary Committee, Roy ignored Indian revolutionaries already working in the Soviet Turkestan. Abdul Rabb Barq had been in Tashkent much before Roy and his colleagues had arrived in Tashkent. They had established the 'Indiskii Dom" or Indian House where Indian revolutionaries lived.[153] Rabb and his colleagues had a different perception of the work at hand.

As Persists remarks, "… Roy's sectarian intolerance was particularly evident during the election of an Organising Committee to convoke the All-India Revolutionary Congress at a general meeting of Indian immigrants. The Committee, under pressure from M. N. Roy and his group, was made of M. N. Roy himself, A. Mukherji and M. Shafiq, that is to say, of Communists only. The leaders of the Association strongly protested at two meetings against such a one Party make-up of the Committee and called for their own representatives to be included in it."

Roy rejected these proposals, saying "the existence of individual groups among the Indian immigrant community must not be encouraged."[154]

The members of the Indian Revolutionary Association were sore at the treatment meted out to them; Roy insisted that they had to be 'subordinated to a centralising unit – the All India Central Revolutionary Committee."

Roy immediately after his arrival in Tashkent had guessed that the new immigrants from India were imbued with the ideology of Pan Islamism and were interested in defending the institution of the Caliphate. Many of them were barely literate and hence, were in no position to appreciate ideological niceties of the doctrines of communism and Marxism. Roy, therefore, sought to allay their fears in an address to them in the month of October 1920. Roy said, "...so, Comrades, you can rest assured that it is not necessary for us Communists to seek for converts. Of course, we are doing, and will always do propaganda to put forth the Communist principles before the Indian masses and the young intellectual revolutionaries. But we don't impose our principles on anybody. The people who tell you that we are trying to make Communists of you forcibly, are nothing but fools and mischief-makers."[155]

But this was hardly reassuring either to the majority of immigrants or to office-bearers of Indian Revolutionary Association.

The programme of the Indian Communist Party formulated by Roy also did not convince the India Revolutionary Association. Roy envisaged a revolution 'that would proclaim the provisional dictatorial authority of an all-Communist Revolutionaries Committee, abolish the national bourgeoisie and end in establishing the power of the proletariat ...'. This stood in sharp contrast to the vision of Indian Revolutionary Association which felt that, 'the only type of revolution that could take place in India in the immediate future was a political revolution, that is, a revolution of national liberation, and only after it and only under certain conditions could preparations for a socialist revolution be started.'[156]

The two factions were ideologically standing on different planes.

Roy offered a sop. On 27 October 1920, the Revolutionary Committee unanimously resolved that Abdur Rabb Barq, the head of the Indian Revolutionary Association, 'be co-opted as an additional member of the Provisional All-India Central Revolutionary Committee.'[157]

But Barq refused to take the bait. He wanted to retain the organisational and political independence of the Indian Revolutionary Association.[158] The conflict intensified.

Expulsion of Barq and Acharya

On a flimsy plea the Revolutionary Committee expelled Rabb

Barq in late November or early December 1920. The Committee recorded its protest to the Soviet authorities in Turkestan for not routing its help to Indian Revolutionary Association through it.[159] The Committee sought to maintain its hegemony by asking the Comintern 'to maintain relations with the Association and other Indian revolutionary forces only through the Central Revolutionary Committee, Tashkent".[160]

Abdur Rabb Barq on 5 December 1920 on behalf of the Association protested against Roy's attitude to Indians not toeing his line. Rabb Barq's letter shows how autocratic Roy was in dealings with his countrymen who held different views. Barq wrote, "There was no need at all to make most of the Indians sign on as hospital guards or become Communists… . We are not against communism, (and) we do not make a difference between a Communist revolutionary or just a revolutionary. All we object to is forcible conversion (to Communism). We have respect for convictions and [we] object to the use of force. Comrade Roy cut off supplies to the Indian Revolutionary Association and immigrants from 3rd instant."[161]

It is hardly surprising that such a behaviour on part of Roy made differences between him and the Indian Revolutionary Association all the more irreconcilable. The Soviet authorities tried to make peace between the two groups. Such an atmosphere bode ill for a united action on part of the Indians.

G. I. Safarov on instructions from ECCI arranged a conciliatory meeting on 22 December 1920. A proposal was mooted to reinstate Rabb Barq but it was turned down on opposition from Roy. At this Acharya resigned declaring "it is impossible for me to work in this Committee any longer with Comrade Roy."[162] The show-down was averted when the Committee refused to accept Acharya's resignation.

It was a deceptive peace. Discontent against Roy continued to simmer.

The tension between the two groups had reached a flash point; a joint meeting of the Turkestan Bureau of the Central Committee of the Russian Communist Party and the Executive of the Central Committee of the Communist Party of the Turkestan was held on 31 December 1920. In this meeting Acharya accused Roy of having coerced immigrants to join the Party. He wanted Roy to 'be dismissed from his job ... in the Indian Revolutionary Committee' because 'he has lost prestige among the Indians.'[163]

The feuding factions were face to face; the mediating body admitted its failure to effect a comprise between them. It suggested to the members of the Revolutionary Committee to proceed to Moscow as soon as possible to solve these issues with the help of Comintern.[164]

Roy precipitated the matters when on 24 January 1921, he along with Abani took a decision to remove Acharya from the membership of the Provisional All India Central Revolutionary Committee. The letter read, "Not only have you in every way sought to hinder the progress of the work, by going from one department to another of the Soviet Government and the International, making groundless accusations against the Committee members and the condition of the Indian work as a whole, but you have done this in an underhanded and sneaking manner, tale-telling, back-biting and otherwise lowering the dignity of the Indian revolutionaries, only coming out before the Committee with your allegations after you have been to several of the Soviet officials."[165]

Roy after sending this communication, removed Acharya from the Chairmanship of the Central Committee of the Indian Communist Party. The letter signed by the Secretary said that the removal was 'on account of actively supporting people engaged in frankly anti-Communist propaganda and on account of bringing groundless accusations against all the party members for which you refused to present any proof.'[166]

Roy proceeded to Moscow early in January 1921 and Acharya and Barq followed him. [167]

The Soviets continued their efforts to resolve the differences between the two groups of Indians amicably. As Persists notes, "The Small Bureau of the Comintern spent several months studying the Indian affairs. A special ECCI Commission of the Turkestan Bureau of the Comintern, consisting of Karl Steinhardt, Konstantin, Zetkin and Ya. Kh. Peters, was sent to Tashkent in

March 1921, for an on-the-spot inquiry. The Commission reported back to Moscow on March 14. A copy of the report was also sent to Lenin and Zinoviev.[168] It stated that it was differences of principle and those of personal relations that were at the root of the conflict. Speaking of the essential differences, it said that the group of Abdur Rabb Barq had accused Roy of an 'erroneous policy of Communist propaganda which is pointless at the present time." In Abdul Barq's opinion, "Nationalism had to be used, too, in considerable measure."[169]

Zetkin and other Committee members reported that 'one hundred and ten men were on their [Roy and Abani] side' and 'the group of Abdur-Rabb consists of eleven members'. The Committee also noted that 'the group of Abdur Rabb is at the least, very liable to suspicion of making secret Pan-Islamist propaganda.' The report also stated, "Pan-Islamist propaganda is a great danger in this country and must be vigorously opposed.'[170]

The Comintern-appointed Commission was inclined to support the Roy faction.

Despite the support received from the investigating committee, Roy was not sure of a favorable decision by the Comintern. So on 19 March 1921 he wrote a letter to Lenin pointing out that Zinoviev harboured feelings of respect for Barq as he held that '...it is undeniable that the Indian Movement cannot be anything but a religio – nationalist anti-British one.'[171] He contested the 'design of Comintern to send back Barq to Tashkent as a member of Indian Revolutionary Committee and requested Lenin to consider his [Roy's] opinion before asking me to go and work with Abdur Rabb there.'[172]

As a last effort to effect a compromise the Comintern-appointed Committee convened a joint meeting at Tashkent of members of the Indian Communist Party, Indian Nationalist Group, Russian Communist Party and staff of the Indian Military School.[173] Abani Mukharjee and Shafiq, the Secretary of the Indian Communist Party accused Rab and Acharya of being in the employment of British Secret Services and insisted that they could not work with Barq and Acharya.[174] As a retaliatory measure Indian Revolutionary Association organised a meeting at Tashkent on 27-4-1921 and passed a resolution inviting Comintern's attention to false accusations being levied by Abani against Barq and Acharya. [175]

The Commission convened joint meetings of both the factions in March and April and suggested setting up a joint committee of both the factions. Barq accepted the proposal but Roy rejected it. Abani supported Roy.[176]

Feud among Indians put the Comintern in a dilemma.

Indians Move to Moscow

In April 1921, the Small Bureau decided to shift Indians to Moscow and place them in the newly-established Communist University of the Toilers of the East.[177] As Roy put it, "the work initiated in Tashkent would henceforth be done more elaborately, on a larger scale, in the Communist University for the Toilers of the East, to be founded in Moscow in the near future."[178] By October 1921, there were eighteen students in the University.[179]

Among the students were several former *muhajirs*, Shaukat Usmani, Gohar Rehman Khan,Rafiq Ahmad, Mohammmed Akbar Shah, Sultan Mehmood, Mir Abdul Majid, Ferozuddin Mansoor, Fida Ali Zahid, Fazl-I-Ilahi Kurban, Abdulla Safdar and others. Soon the number grew to 30. A working Committee consisting of Mohammed Shafiq, Abani Mkerjee and M.N.Roy looked after the Indian students. (Dmitriev, *Indian…In Central Asia*, p.125)

Roy has given a graphic account of the closure of the Military School. He arrived in Tashkent and convened a meeting of all Indian immigrants and told them about the decision to close down the School.

The decision was also influenced by the fact that the number of Indian students did not increase as expected. The flow of Indian immigrants also started tapering off as freedom movement in India lost its momentum when the Non-Co-operation was called off and Mustafa Kemal Ataturk abolished the Caliphate. Some trainess were also drafted for propaganda work and taken off the School. Nevertheless the proposed closure did disappoint the Indian students.(Ibid.,p.124) This can be seen from Roy's statement. He says, "the perspective of Indian Centre in Tashkent being broken up in the near future seemed to cause a great deal of anxiety to those concerned. But few volunteered to return to India to participate in the anti-British movement there."[180] Eventually a decision was taken about what the inmates would do.

According to Roy, "Some of them would settle down in Tashkent and take to small trade to earn their livelihood. Others would try their luck in Persia and Afghanistan, if they were given some money to help. The more adventurous few would take the risk of reaching the North-Western frontier of India through the no-man's land of Eastern Bokhara". [181]

Money was distributed among Indians and 'different groups of non-political majority left on their way back, respectively chosen by themselves.'[182]

The closure of the Military School and the decision to carry on propaganda activity from Moscow in place of Tashkent meant that Moscow alone was to be the focal point of all revolutionary Indians in the Soviet Union.

The Military School, while it functioned, drew a good number of Indians. "The first group of 11 trainees was enrolled for the aviation section. They began their training on 12 November 1920.In January 1921 a machinegun infantry section was also opened up in which there were 18 Indian trainees. A preparatory section was also organized which had a strength of 12 trainees. The chief of the training courses was a former Captain of the Tsarist army, G.N. Frolov, who was the Head of Tashkent School for Military Officers.The Chief of the training programme was Lt. Col. S.I. Kolomeitsev, lecturer of the Tashkent Cadet Corps. The political and party work among the trainees was looked after by the Commissar, A.M.Tarakanov, a member of the RCP(B) since 1917, a former deputy of the Moscow Soviet and Chairman of the party cell, I.P.Marchenko."[183]

Indians received training in artillery, tactics, fortification, and use of machinegun. They were also taught Russian and English languages.[184]

The Indian students were satisfied with the training they received. One of them later recalled, 'the military school gave to its students besides military, political education as well." (Ibid.)

Some of these students later on served in the Soviet armed forces with distinction.

With the closure of the Military School in May1921[185] Tashkent ceased to be a Soviet -sponsored base for Indian freedom fighters.

Indians intending to visit the Soviet Union from Afghanistan continued to pass through Tashkent. Rahmat Ali Zakaria, a member of the Indian Provisional Government in Kabul was one such Indian.[186]

The change over to Moscow did not end the bitterness among Indians.

Allegations and counter-allegations were hurled against each other by Indians belonging to different factions which only undermined the credibility of Indian patriots.

The Berlin group was not very happy with the formation of the Indian Communist Party at Tashkent. Roy himself concedes this and refers to the criticism levelled against the ICP by GAK Luhani, a spokesman of the Berlin Committee who had come to Moscow to attend the Third Congress of the Comintern in 1921.[187] But Abani in Tashkent continued to woo the Berlin group so as to prevent them from supporting Barq and Acharya.[188]

The opponents could not convince the Comintern about their stand against Roy.

Roy's group was recognised as the Communist Party of India on the recommendation of an Indian Commission formed by the Small Bureau of Comintern in June 1921 under the Chairmanship of a Dutch Communist S. J. Rutgers.[189]

While the two groups were busy trying to impose their point of view on each other, some political work was also being carried out, especially outside Tashkent. Bukhara and Andijan had substantial number of Indians. According to one calculation there were 200 Indians residing in Bukhara in March 1922.[190] They were roughly divided into groups. One group had arrived during the First World War and owed allegiance to the Provisional Government of Independent India in Kabul. The other was that of *muhajirins*, who had come after the *Khilafat* agitation began in India. The *muhajirins* continued to come to Bukhara even in

1922. When Bukhara became a republic, a "Provisional Indian Revolutionary Committee" consisting of Gulam Mohammed, Gulam Rbbani and Faizullah Mahmud was formed. The idea was to unite both the segments of the Indians.[191]

The Bukharans sent a delegation to Tashkent headed by Mohammad Ali, a Communist and a close friend of M.N. Roy. It seems nothing came out of it.[192] The Indians in Tashkent were in disarray after they had been shifted to Moscow. Secondly, The Bukharan Indians in their approach were closer to the position of "Indian Revolutionary Association' and its leader Abdur Rab. However, the services of Indian immigrants were utilized by the Republic of Bukhara in many capacities. Those having skill in languages were put in the Ministry of External Affairs. Some were put in telephone exchanges; a section of Indians joined the machine gun section of the Red Army and the militia in Bukhara.[193] Some of the Indians, not enthusiastic about the Soviet system proceeded to the Kemalist Turkey.[194]

In 1922 Maulana Obeidullah Sindhi, a member of the Indian Provisional Government in Kabul arrived in Bukhara along with his nine associates. He was a Pan Islamist and he proceeded to Moscow and Leningrad. He met the Russian Foreign Minister Chicherin but eventually proceeded to Turkey.[195]

Andijan like Tashkent and Bukhara had a substantial Indian population. After the Bolshevik Revolution, the Soviets tried to win them over. The Soviet organs recognized it 'as an organization of foreign residents.' Its members in 1919 publicaly announced their support for the Soviet power.[196] On the direction of the Provisional Revolutionary Committee, M.T.Acharya was sent to Andijan to work among the local Indian Community and to recruit some of them as cadets in the Military School and to contact Kashgar rebels and also to find a safe route for revolutionaries to go to India. Shaukat Usmani followed him. After Usmani reached Andijan, Acharya returned to Tashkent.[197]

These revolutionaries persuaded twenty Andijan Indians to join the ranks of revolutionaries. Fifteen Indians were sent to study in the 'Soviet and Party School' in Tashkent and the Turkestan School of the Trade Unions.[198]

Undoubtedly the Revolutionary ferment affected Indians in major cities of Central Asia.

More Indian Revolutionaries in Tashkent

Indians based in Tahkent also tried to maintain and develop contacts with Kabul to further the revolutionary work. Some of the Indians set out for India to carry on their propaganda work against British colonialism and capitalism. They were asked to speak in favour of Communism and the Soviet Union.

Sheikh Abdul Haque who had come to Tashkent as a representative of the "Indian Liberation League" a Kabul-based organisation while going back with money was arrested by the Afghan Government on a charge of being a British Agent.[199]

Mohammad Ali reached Kabul in the spring of 1921 where he met Indian immigrants. The Russian envoy F. F. Raskolnikov helped him in sending articles and other material about the Soviet Union for publication in newspapers in North India.[200] Mohammad Ali sent to Ahmedabad session of the Indian National Congress the programme prepared by M. N. Roy.[201] He also impressed Mota Singh, an Indian revolutionary who had arrived in Kabul to escape British repression, to go back and try to form a Communist Party on the Indian soil.[202]

Mohammad Shafiq, the Secretary of the Indian Communist Party in Tashkent also reached Kabul in 1921. He helped Mohammad Ali in forging links with the Indian National Congress, whose branch was established in Kabul in 1921.[203] These Communists in Afghanistan felt that Gandhi was the darling of the Indian masses. They toned down their opposition to him and described him 'as the greatest national leader of the Indian masses'.[204] Geographical proximity to the Indian soil, interaction with different sections of Indian society, enabled them to correctly assess Indian political realities as compared to leaders like M.N. Roy or Abani Mukerjee, who had been away from the country for a very long time and were not in touch with ground realities.

In early 1922, thirteen Indian revolutionaries left Tashkent for India via the Pamirs in small groups via different routes. Unfortunately on arrival, within a short span of time, they were all arrested; the British government instituted the "Moscow-Tashkent conspiracy case."[205]

Barkatullah, the Prime Minister of the Provisional Government of India in Kabul accompanied Mahendra Pratap to Central Asia and Moscow after the Soviet regime was established. In 1919 the went to the Soviet Union as an emissary of King Amanullah of Afghanistan. He never became a Communist. He propagated the Socialist ideals among the Muslims in Central Asia from Tashkent. He earned the respect of top leaders of the Soviet Union. He left the Soviet Union in 1922 and settled down in Berlin.[206] He remained in touch with the Soviets in Geneva and Berlin but had dissociated himself from Communism.

The most important Indian to have come to Tashkent from Afghanistan was Maulana Obaidullah Sindhi, a member of the Provisional Government. After the Afghan King Amanullah expelled the Provisional Government in 1922, Obaidullah decided to journey via Soviet Central Asia on way to Constantinople. The Soviet Government accorded him permission to travel across its territory and allowed him to stay on the Soviet soil as long as he wished.[207] He was accompanied by a number of young men among whom was Shibdas Banerjee alias Abdul.[208]

By 1922 the Soviets had lost interest in developing Tashkent as a base for helping Indian patriots in their anti- British activities. Their international interests became paramount. While the Capitalist countries had failed in their military adventures on the Soviet soil, the Bolsheviks had also not succeeded in stirring up an international proletarian revolution. However the Soviets continued to help India's freedom struggle from Moscow though in a clandestine manner. Moscow and not Tashkent was to become the hub of Indian activities.

One may speculate why Tashkent failed to develop into a major centre for Indian revolutionaries. Many reasons can be advanced.

The Indian revolutionaries who had come together in Tashkent, as has been shown earlier, were a heterogeneous lot both politically and ideologically. As Barq pointed out, "The sole attraction for the Indian revolutionaries is the revolutionary spirit in Russia, its contiguity to India & its being a revolutionary school for the young revolutionaries." They were not communists. Many of them did not like the atheist Marxist ideology. Much to their chagrin, they had to work under the orders of Comintern. As Barq said, "The Komintern pays no attention to their representations and demands complete submission to its dictates." This was just not possible because as Barq noted, "A Revolutionary is a revolutionary simply because he is fighting for self determination. If he accepts dictatorship of friend or foe he is no revolutionary but a mean adventurer or a dangerous spy."[209] Hence, conflicts arose between those who toed the Comintern line and those who tried to differ from it. Ideology shaped and nurtured differene of opinion to the point of open conflict.

Relationship became bitter when the Comintern bureaucracy treated those who adopted an independent attitude with contempt and even stopped supplying them necessities of life. Barq alleged that he and his supporters were deprived of means of sustenance and had to 'live by selling their clothes.'[210]

Rabb had held fast to his view even while deposing before the Indian Commission which met on 6/8/1921 under Rutgers. He had complained 'The Communists make intrigues in an association which is not their own and insult the noncommunists for their religious beliefs.'[211] The atheist Marxist doctrine could not win over Indians, most of whom were *muhajirins* and who had left the country with the sole object of fighting for the survival of the institution of the Caliphate.

Rabb and Acharya also lost the sympathy of the Comintern because of their non-compromising attitude. Mahendra Pratap who was in Moscow, portrayed both of them, in a letter dated December 1921, 'as quarrelsome and given to intrigues'. On their conduct in Kabul he said, "Having gained the confidence of Comrades Suritz and Reisner [Russian diplomats in Kabul] Messers Abdur Rabb and Achariya after our arrival in Kabul, began to play their destructive game against me without any regard for decency or veracity'. He went on to say, " They [Rabb and Acharya], with the help of Soviet money, brought together a number of Indians in Kabul and made a show of revolutionary organization. Since they were living in the Russian embassy, their behaviour was responsible, to a large extent, for the estrangement between [the] Soviet [s] and Afghanistan early in 1920 A. D. and consequently as well for the going of the Afghan mission to India to negotiate Anglo-Afghan treaty."[212]

Another important factor was the nature of Indian emigrants present in Tashkent. Most of Indians whom Roy, Acharya and Rabb Barq tried to organise into 'Indian Liberation Army' were *muhajirins* imbued with the idea of Pan Islamism and a desire to fight for the Caliphate. Religiosity and not revolutionary nationalism had brought them to Tashkent. Even an year's work could not wean them away from Pan Islamist ideals. Attempts to inculcate Marxist ideology did not succeed because of the social background of the immigrant Indian community.

Why Tashkent had to be Abandoned

The Communist propaganda preached social revolution, class-war, proletarian internationalism and atheism, concepts which most of them, barely literate, could hardly appreciate. It is not surprising as Persists notes, "when Indian communists set up three-week classes of history, economics, problems of the working-class movement and socialism in Tashkent, they found no students to attend them."[213] Persists continues, the reason was that Indians considered a 'a knowledge of political economy and social science… against their religion, and there were no registrations for these classes, but only for the language class'.[214]

The Indian immigrants also felt disillusioned and confused because of the factional feuding among the leadership.

Above all, the whole idea of liberating India by creating an army was utopian. Roy and his Indian companions had been out of India for so long that they had lost touch with Indian realities. The Comintern and Soviet officials based their assessment on scanty reports on India published in Central European Press. They read about the Non-co-operation Movement and thought that a general upsurge had taken place in India. They, therefore, thought that an organised army would be able to push out the British colonial rulers. How naïve was this assessment! Roy later on realised his naivette. He wrote, "Scrappy news of that [Non-co-operation] movement had reached Moscow through the intermediary of the British Press, which played it down. Very little of that news appeared in the European continental press. On the basis of these scanty indirect reports, the Russian papers had manufactured stories about the powerful mass revolutionary movement against British imperialism in India. I had myself written a number of these stories, which were read eagerly as authentic and authoritative reports of the situation. But none more than myself deplored the inadequacy of reliable information and my ignorance of what was actually happening in India."[215]

Finally, the British ruling circles also forced the Bolsheviks to stop rendering aid to Indian revolutionaries gathered in Tashkent. The British ruling class was agitated on hearing the news about the Tashkent Military School where Indian patriots were receiving military training. The fiery speeches made at the inaugural session of the School had been reported to Lord Curzon who sent on ultimatum to the Soviet government to desist from such acts which, he claimed, 'jeopardised' the security of India.

Withdrawal of Soviet Support to Indians in Tashkent

Krassin, had on behalf of the Soviet government opened negotiations for a trade agreement with the British Prime Minister Lloyd George on 31 May 1920.It was finally signed on 21 March 1921 '..., in effect [it] constituted *de facto* recognition by Great Britain of the Soviet government, the regime which the British tried to obliterate at its inception'.[216] A clause in the Agreement read, "That each Party refrains from hostile actions or undertaking against the other and from conducting outside of its own borders any official propaganda, direct or indirect, against the institutions of the British Empire or the Russian Soviet Republic respectively, and more particularly that the Russian Soviet Government refrains from any attempt, by military or diplomatic or by any other form of action or propaganda to encourage any other peoples of Asia in any form of hostile action against British interest or British Empire, especially in India and the Independent state of Afghanistan."[217]

The conclusion of the Agreement was accompanied by a letter presented by Sir Robert Horne, President of the Board of Trade which enumerated in detail the activities of Indian revolutionaries both in Kabul and Tashkent and the support extended to them by various Soviet authorities. It said "...upon the cessation of which His Majesty's Government must insist as an essential corollary of the conclusion of any agreement between the two governments."[218]

The content of the letter indicated that the British were well aware of what the Indian revolutionaries were doing and also what moral and material aids were being offered to them by the Soviets. The British intelligence system had successfully penetrated into the network of Indian revolutionaries. It now sought to invoke the clause of this agreement to force the Soviets to withdraw their support to the Indian freedom fighters. The Soviets already fed up with the internecine quarrels of Indian revolutionaries and fearful of British cancellation of the Agreement decided to accord precedence to the interest of the Soviet government and not to Soviet ideology. The Military School at Tashkent was closed as Sehnavis said on account of the pressure of the British government.[219] The Trade Agreement was the occasion and not the cause.

The Soviets had realised that dreams of creating an Indian liberation army invading India through Afghanistan were utopian since Afghanistan was not inclined to permit either personnel or war-material through its territory to the North-Western borders of India. If arms could not be sent to India a military uprising was unthinkable.

Indian revolutionaries failed to fashion a unanimous leadership. Indians though sincere in their outrage against the British were never united about either the strategy or the leadership; their schemes were impractical.

At the same time the Soviets had quickly learnt their lessons. Experience of international politics had taught them that real politik and ideology seldom went together. Therefore, the Soviets decided to forgo the chimera of 'world revolution' and sought to consolidate 'the revolution in one country'. This meant, to please the British, the abandonment of Tashkent as a military base and disallowing of its use to Indians for waging their war of liberation against the British rule. The Indians had no option but to accept the orders of the Soviet Government.

The Soviet decision caused problems for Indian revolutionaries staying in Tashkent.

Many Indians were not in a position to return to their country where they faced arrest, police and legal harassment. Such Indians accepted the Soviet offer to shift to Moscow. Some of the Indians were admitted to various military academies; the rest joined KUTV (the newly established University for the Toiling Workers of the East); others hoped they could return to India. Nevertheless Indian revolutionaries quit Tashkent.

The Soviet decision, at this distance of time, appears to have been realistic in the light of events which unfolded in Afghanistan, Turkey and India.

In October 1922 the Afghan ruler Aamanullah succumbed to British pressure and asked the Provisional Government to quit the Afghan territory. Maulana Obaidullah was asked to leave; he chose to go to Constantinople via Tashkent and Moscow; the Soviets conceded his request.[220]

On 12 February 1922 Gandhi called off the Non-Cooperation Movement.[221] The assessment of M. N. Roy that India was in the grip of mass upheaval was not correct. Swayed by this analysis Roy had told the Indian National Congress, "let it make the immediate demands of the Trade Unions, as summarized by the Cawnpur workers, its own demands; let it make the programme of Kissan Sabha [Peasant Organisation] its own programme, and time will soon come when the Congress will not stop before any obstacle; ...".[222] His advice had no meaning for Indian political leaders who were conducting the struggle and who understood the Indian situation much better than Roy did. India was quiet once Gandhi withdrew the movement. Chances of an immediate socialist revolution had receded.

Finally, in Turkey Kamal Pasha abolished the Caliphate and the Khilafat movement in India lost its *raison d'etre*. The Muslim anger against the British rule subsided. Objectively speaking once the British rule in India was no longer menaced by internal rebellion, the chances to trigger it from far off Tashkent were almost nil.

In the fourth Congress of Comintern held in November 1922, the Congress Chairman Zinonoviev and its Secretary Karl Radek paid glowing tributes to Roy and his colleague.[223] They had reached a different conclusion. A secret Comintern document signed by Stalin and Ter-Avanesoff noted, "A mistake was made by the Communist International in its first efforts to promote a revolution in India. Far too much credence has been given to the assurances of the delegates of the small Communist Parties of the East to the Third congress in regard to the preparedness of the Asiatic people to adopt Communism. The real aspirations of these peoples to emancipate themselves from the foreign yoke were consequently used merely as an argument to induce them to accept communism. It has now been realized that Communism is completely unacceptable to the Hindus in their present state of development, and independence is a condition which must precede it. Our propaganda agents did not realize this and did not report it and continued to work completely on wrong lines."[224] It went on to admit that an 'enquiry into the tactics it [Comintern] had employed in Central Asia and Asia during the year 1921' had resulted in the conclusion 'that the work of the propaganda agents had yielded no results whatsoever…'.[225]

A Commission of Enquiry set up by the Comintern consisting of Zinoviev, Eliawa and Vosnessensky 'confirmed the inefficiency and uselessness of these propaganda schools [at Tashkent and Samarkand]' though it said that Comrade Vosnessensky had succeeded 'in sending fifteen properly trained agents to the most important centres in India and Afghanistan, but this is quite out of proportion to the magnitude of the task'.[226] We hope someday we will know who these people were.

After the Comintern reversed its policy, occasionally Indian patriots could sneak into Tashkent either via Afghanistan or the Pamir Plateau but neither in Tashkent nor in Kabul they posed any threat to the stability of the British rule in India. The British intelligence kept British Indian authorities well informed about what was going on in among Indian revolutionaries in Tashkent and Kabul.

This is evident from the Curzon ultimatum sent to the Soviet Union on 8 May 1923 which claimed that in November 1922, seven Indians trained in Tashkent as agitators had been arrested on their arrival in India.[227] It further noted that Raskolnikov, the Soviet representative in Kabul had implored the authorities not to curtail his "Indian work and extraordinary expenses", since such a step would cause 'an irretrievable loss to the work of the legation in its vital spheres.'[228]

The Soviets paid full attention to British complaints and British wishes. For reasons of State they did not want to incur British displeasure. They once again agreed, "To refrain from hostile action or undertakings against Great Britain, and from conducting outside of its borders any official propaganda direct or indirect against the institutions of British Empire, and more particularly to refrain from any attempt by military or diplomatic or any other form of action or propaganda to encourage any of the peoples of Asia in any form of hostile action against British interests or the British Empire, especially in India and in the independent state of Afghanistan."[229]

As a gesture of Soviet good faith, the Soviet government recalled its envoy Raskolnikov from Afghanistan, a known supporter of Indian revolutionaries.

The Soviets, however, did not totally abandon India. Though convinced that Tashkent or Afghanistan would not be the places from where to conduct an ideological war against British India, they decided to develop a new route Moscow-Berlin, in place of Moscow-Tashkent-Kabul line. The Treaty of Rapallo signed between the Soviet Union and Germany in 1922 had paved the possibility of developing this route. M. N. Roy in 1922 shifted to Berlin from where he conducted his propaganda in favour of Communism by publishing a series of papers till his expulsion by Comintern in 1928.

Conclusion

For a brief period of five years, from the aftermonth of the Bolshevik Revolution of 1917 to 1922 Tashkent remained an important centre of activity of Indian patriots who were determined to oust the British rulers from India. The Soviet support was a crucial factor in the emergence of Tashkent as a base for anti-British struggle.

Two factors inhibited Indian efforts from becoming effective. First, Indians coming from a variety of socio-economic background and motivated by different factors in their opposition to the British rule, failed to evolve a common strategy and could not throw up a leader acceptable to Indians of all hues. It seems that internal bickering among Indians enabled British spies to monitor their activities and inform the British government. The colonial power was in a position to take suitable defensive measures and impede the propaganda work of agents of Comintern.

It is also true that the Soviet Government had to bow before the pressure exerted by the British Government in order to ensure its acceptability in the international arena. Bowing to the British demands, it withdrew material support given to Indian patriots based in Tashkent. The Bolsheviks asked them to shift to Moscow. The Indians had no option but to agree to the decision of the Soviet authorities. However, several Indian patriots during their stay in Tashkent had the chance to study Marxism and also to obtain a first hand experience of its working in underdeveloped Asian Countries. Some were convinced of its effectiveness as a major tool in their struggle against their colonial British masters. On return to India, they became propagators of Marxist doctrines and as members of the Communist Party of India they tried to organise peasants in the countryside and industrial workers in the urban areas and added new dimensions to Indian struggle for freedom.

The Soviets and the Comintern did not completely write off Tashkent as a conduit for instigating uprising in India against British rule. British Intelligence Reports suggest that in January 1924, once again, talk was afoot to establish the headquarters of the "Near-Central Eastern Section" of the Comintern at Tashkent 'with a sum of 1,000,000 gold roubles. Half of this amount was for use in India and on her border'.[230] It did not materialize.

Indians in Tashkent despite their failure to bring about a

military uprising against British rule in India wrote a shining chapter in the freedom struggle of their country.

Footnotes

1. Devendra Kaushik, "India and Central Asia : Political Contacts from Colonial Period to Aftermath of the Socialist Revolution" in Surendra Gopal(ed), *India and Central Asia (*Delhi, 2001), pp.99-138.
2. C.S.Samra, *India and Anglo-Soviet Relations (*1917-1947) (Bombay,1959), pp.3-19.
3. G.L.Dmitriyev, "From the History of Indian Colony in Central Asia" in *India and Central Asia,* pp.95-96.
4. Mahendra Pratap, *My Life Story Of Fifty five Years,* (Delhi , 1974), p.55
5. Ibid.
6. T.N. Zagorodnikova and P.M.Shastitko (chief eds), *Russko-ndiiskiye Otnosheniya v 1900-1917 gg.(Moscow, 1999),* Doc. No.323.
   Hereafter cited as *R-I.O.v1900-1917 gg.*
7. Ibid., Doc. No. 324
8. Ibid., Doc. No. 325
9. Ibid., Doc. No. 326
10. Ibid., Doc. No. 328
11. Ibid., Doc. Nos. 329 and 330
12. Ibid., Doc. No. 329
13. Ibid., Doc. No. 331
14. Ibid., Doc. No. 333
15. Ibid., Doc. No. 334
16. The real name of Shamsher Singh was Dr. Mathura Singh. Pratap, p.55
17. Ibid.
18. *R-I. O.v 1900-1917 gg.*, Doc. No. 334.
19. Ibid., Doc. No.335
20. Ibid., Doc. No.336
21. Ibid., Doc. No.337
22. Ibid., p. 458 f.n. 12
23. Ibid., Doc. Nos. 338 and 339
24. Ibid., Doc. No. 339
25. Ibid., Doc. No. 340
26. Pratap, p. 57

27. *R-I-O.v. 1900-1917gg., Doc. No. 341*
28. Pratap. p. 57
29. *R-I-O.v. 1900-1917gg.,* Doc. No. 342
30. Ibid.
31. Ibid.
32. Pratap, p. 57; *R-I.O.v 1900-1917gg.,* p. 459 f.n. 15
33. M.A. Persists, "Eastern Internationalists in Russia And Some Questions of the National Liberation Movement (1918-July 1920)" in Ulyanovsky (ed.), *The Comintern and the East* (Moscow, 1979), p. 77.
34. Ibid. pp. 21-22
35. Ibid. p.24
36. Bailey, *Mission to Tashkent* (London, 1946); Etherton, *In The Heart of Asia* (London, 1925)
37. Samra, p. 25
38. Bailey, p.
39. M.A. Persists, "Eastern Internationalists in Russia And Some Questions of the National Liberation Movement (1918-July 1920)" in Ulyanovsky (ed.), *The Comintern and the East* (Moscow, 1979), p. 84.
40. Ibid., p. 85
41. Ibid., p.83
42. Ibid.
43. Samra, p. 24
44. A.V. Raikov, *Probuzhdeniye Indii* (Moscow, 1968), p. 136. Besides meeting Lenin, they also met Y.M. Sverdlov, the President.
45. Persists, loc. cit., p.81
46. T. R. Sareen, *British Intervention In Central Asia And Trans-Caucasia,* (New Delhi, 1989), Chs.3 and 4.
47. Dietrich Reetz, *Hijrat : The flight of the Faithful A British file on the Exodus of Muslim Peasants from North India to Afghanistan* : 1920, (Berlin, 1995), p. 18
48. Ibid.
49. Ibid., p. 22 ; Samra, pp. 38-39. Amanullah gave this call on 4 May 1919.
50. Ibid., p. 32
51. Samra, p. 41
52. *Zulqarnain, 28 July 1920* quoted in Reetz, p. 39. f. n. 123
53. Reetz, p. 41
54. Ibid., p. 43

55. Ibid., p. 46
56. Ibid.
57. Ibid., pp. 46-47
58. Ibid., p. 48
59. Ibid., p. 51
60. Ibid., p. 53
61. Ibid., pp. 68-69
62. Ibid., p. 69
63. Shaukat Usmani, *Historic Trips of a Revolutionary : Sojourn in the Soviet Union* (Delhi 1977), p. 6
64. Ibid.
65. S.M.Mehdi, *The Story behind 'Moscow-Tashkent Conspiracy Case?' (Delhi, 1967), pp. 10-11*
66. Usmani, p. 21
67. Ibid., Chapter 3
68. Ibid., pp. 25-26
69. Ibid., pp. 27-33
70. Ibid., pp. 35-36
71. Reetz, p. 43, f.n. 132
72. S.M.Mehdi, p. 11
73. Ibid.
74. A. B. Reznikov, "The Comintern's Oriental Policy" in R. A. Ulyanvosky(ed.), *The Comintern and the East A Ciritique of the Critique*(Moscow, 1978), p. 39
75. Purabi Roy, Sobhanlal Datta Gupta and Hari Vasudevan (eds.), *Indo- Russian Relations 1917-1947, Part I 1917-1928*(henceforth quoted as *I-RR,* Calcutta, 1999), Doc No.6
76. *M.N.Roy, Memoirs* (Bombay, 1964) henceforth cited as *Memoirs* p. 390
77. Ibid., p. 391
78. Ibid.
79. Samra, p. 48; Raikov, p.137. According to Roy a number of Indian soldiers who had deserted the British army in Khorasan had reached Baku. They were hailed as delegates to the Baku Congress. *Memoirs,* p. 395
80. Samra, pp. 48-49
81. Ibid., 49
82. *Memoirs,* p. 392
83. Samra, p. 53. Unfortunately, the names of Indians and the places from where they came are not available to us.
84. Samra, pp. 53-54

85. Ibid., p.54
86. Ibid., pp. 55-56
87. *Memoirs*, p. 414
88. Ibid., p. 417
89. Ibid.
90. Ibid., p. 435
91. Ibid.
92. Ibid.
93. Ibid., p. 436
94. Ibid.
95. Ibid., pp. 436-37
96. Ibid., p.437
97. Ibid.
98. Ibid., p. 457
99. Ibid.
100. Ibid., pp. 462-63
101. Ibid., p. 463
102. Ibid., p. 465
103. Purabi Roy, Sobhanlal Gupta and Hari Vasudevan (eds.), *Indo-Russian Relations*, *1917-1947*, Part I, (Calcutta, 1999), Doc No.22.
104. Ibid., p. 40
105. Ibid., p. 41
106. Ibid., pp. 41-42
107. Ibid., p.42-43
108. Ibid., p. 43
109. *Revolutionaries of India...*, p. 178
110. *Indo-Russian Relations* 1917-47, Part I, Doc. , No. 23
111. Ibid.
112. Ibid.
113. Ibid., doc. No. 24
114. Ibid., Doc. No. 25
115. Ibid., p. 53
116. Ibid., p.54
117. Ibid., p. 55
118. Ibid., Doc. No. 27
119. Ibid., p. 57
120. Shaukat Usmani, p. 49
121. Ibid.
122. Ibid., p. 51
123. M. A. Persists, *Revolutionaries of India in Soviet Russia* (Moscow, 1973), p. 219

124. Ibid.
125. Ibid.
126. Ibid.
127. Ibid., p. 220
128. Ibid., p. 220
129. Mehdi, p. 23
130. Usmani, p. 71-72
131. Mehdi, p.20
132. *Memoirs*, Ch. 63
133. Ibid., p. 470
134. *Indian Revolutionaries in Russia...,* pp. 238-401
135. *Indian Revolutionaries in Russia..*, p.241; Simultaneously the office of the Eastern Section of Comintern at Tashkent was closed down. It was a clear signal that Comintern was no longer keen to develop Tashkent as a base for its support to Indian Revolutionaries. Usmani, p. 66.
136. *Indian Revolutionaries in Russia...,* p. 240
137. Ibid.
138. *Memoirs,* p. 467
139. Shaukat Usmani, p. 52
140. Muzaffar Ahmad mentions Masood Ali Shah. Muzaffar Ahmad, *Myself and the Communist Party of India* (Calcutta, 1970), pp. 297-98
141. *Indo-Russian Relations in 1917-27,* Part I, Doc No. 70
142. *Memoirs*, p.p. 435-36
143. Ibid., pp. 463-64, 473
144. Ibid., p. 473
145. Ibid.
146. Ibid., p. 474
147. Ibid., p. 475
148. Mehdi, p. 32
149. Shaukat Usmani, p. 47
150. *Revolutionaries od India...,* p. 116
151. Ibid., p. 122
152. Ibid., p.169
153. Ibid., p.175
154. Ibid., p. 176
155. Ibid., p. 204
156. Ibid., p.180
157. Ibid., p. 176
158. Ibid., pp. 176-77

159. *Indo-Russian Relations* 1917-47, Part I, Doc. No. 23
160. Ibid., p. 177
161. Ibid., p. 204
162. Ibid.
163. Ibid., p. 205
164. Ibid., pp. 205-6
165. *Indo-Russian Relations 1917-1928,* Part I, Doc. No.28
166. Ibid., Doc. No. 29
167. Ibid., p.206
168. *Indo-Russian Relations 1917-1928,* Part I, Doc.No.30
169. *Indian Revolutionaries*, p. 206
170. Ibid., p.60
171. *Indo-Russian Relations 1917-1928*, Part I, Doc. No. 31
172. Ibid.
173. Ibid., Doc. No.32
174. Ibid.
175. Ibid., Doc. No. 33
176. Ibid., p. 206 ; *Indo-Russian Relations 1917-1927...,* Doc. No. 5
177. Ibid., p. 206 ; The decision to established the University was taken on 21 April 1921, *Memoirs,* p. 528
178. Memoirs, p. 532
179. Ibid., p. 208.
180. Memoirs, p. 528
181. Ibid.
182. Ibid.
183. Dmitriev, *Indian Revolutionaries... Central Asia*, p.123
184. Ibid.
185. Ibid., p.125
186. *Indo-Russia Relations* 1917-27, Part I, Doc No. 209
187. *Memoirs*, p. 490
188. *Indo-Russia Relations* 1917-27, Part I, Doc No.34
189. Ibid., p. 212
190. Dmitriev, *Indian Revolutionaries ...Central Asia*, p.125
191. Ibid., p.126
192. Ibid.,p.126
193. Ibid., pp.126-27
194. Ibid.,p.127
195. Ibid., pp.127-28
196. Dmitriev, *Indian Revolutionaries ... Central Asia*, p.121
197. Sehnavis, p. 148
198. Dmitriev, *Indian Revolutionaries In Central Asia* , p.121

199. *Indo-Russia Relations* 1917-27, Part I, p. 73
200. *Indo-Russia Relations* 1917-27, p. 221
201. Ibid.
202. Ibid., p. 222
203. Ibid.
204. Ibid., p. 223
205. Ibid., p. 224
206. *Indo-Russia Relations* : 1917-28, Doc No. 90, p. 374-75
207. *Memoirs*, pp. 491-492
208. Chinmoy Sehanavis, *RusBiplab Pravasi Bhartiya Biplabi(in Bengalee)*, Calcutta, 1973, p.187
209. *Indo-Russian Relations;*1917-27, Doc. No.36
210. Ibid., p. 81
211. Ibid., p. 140
212. Ibid., Doc. No. 56
213. *Indian Revolutionaries..., p. 195*
214. Ibid.
215. Memoirs, pp. 540-41
216. Samra, p. 56
217. Ibid., p.57
218. Ibid., pp. 57-61
219. Sehnavis, p. 163
220. Samra, p. 97
221. Samra, p. 65
222. Ibid., p. 63
223. Samra, pp. 66-67
224. Ibid., p.68
225. Samra, p. 69
226. Ibid.
227. Ibid., pp. 75-76
228. Samra, pp. 76-77
229. Ibid., p 80
230. Ashoke Kumar Mukhopadhyay (ed), *India And Communism Secret Documents* (Calcutta, 1997), p. 28

A Little Known Chapter

Indians in Central Asia from Mid-1920s to 1940s

Indian patriots had, even, in the nineteenth century used Anglo-Russian contradictions to further the cause of their country's deliverance from the British yoke.[1] The tradition continued when the Bolshevik government replaced the Tsarist administration in Central Asia in the aftermath of the November Revolution of 1917. As has been shown earlier, for a brief period, it seemed Tashkent would emerge as a major center of emigrant Indian freedom fighters as the Bolshevik rule, motivated partly by ideological reasons and partly by their desire to put pressure on the British Government which had militarily intervened in the Civil War on the side of White Russians and the monarchists, supported Indian freedom fighters in all possible ways. Indians welcomed Bolshevik initiative who spoke of 'proletarian internationalism' and were committed to wipe out 'colonialism' and 'capitalism'. They had hopes that Indian patriots would oust their British rulers.[2] In 1920, they established the Tashkent Military School to train Indians in the use of modern weaponry; in the same year M.N.Roy, Abani Mukharji, and others set up Indian Communist Party in Tashkent to propagate communism among Indians. Soon the Bolsheviks in pursuit of their wider international interests changed their policies; the School was closed down and the Indians were asked to enroll in the newly established University for the Toilers of East in Moscow.[3]

Indians dispersed. Some went to Bukhara; some moved towards Turkey; some left for Chinese-held Eastern Turkestan where an Indian trading community was well entrenched in Kashgar, Yarkand, Khotan, etc. The flow of freedom fighters fleeing India and entering Central Asia through Afghanistan or

Chinese Turkestan stopped. Tashkent was no longer a major concentration point of Indians, traders or freedom fighters.

However some Indians remained in Central Asia. They were petty shop-keepers or small job-holders. They continued to live in Soviet Cetrasl Asia till 1936 when the government enforced full-scale 'collectivisation of economy'. This is confirmed by the fact that Indians continued to be repatriated to Afghanistan till 1930s. Markowits cites the cases of Lala and Nicha who arrived in Kandhar in 1931 and registered their claims with the British Consul in December 1931. In their petition they stated that they had lost everything when the Soviet armed forces captured Bukhara in 1920.They were taken to Samarkand as prisoners and released after an year.They then returned to Bukhara and raised a small loan to start a business in order to earn their living. It seems that their business prospered and they accumulated capital, between 60,000 and 70,000 rupees, quite a sum in those days. Thereafter they decided to return to India.[4]

Occasional Indians trying to escape from the British rule reached here because Indians sneaked into Afghanistan through its porus border and then reached Central Asia by crossing the river Oxus.

For all practical purposes Indian immigration to Central Asia ceased in mid-1920s. Thus stopped a process which had been going on almost uninterrupted for the last several centuries.

Indians temporarily stopped going to Central Asia in mid-1920s but since they were still welcome in Moscow they took the alternative route of going to the USSR via Iran across the Caspian Sea to Baku and then to Moscow. But they still entertained the desire to go to Central Asia and see how communism had transformed a predominantly illiterate Muslim country into a forward-looking modern nation where agriculture had been mechanized, religious and racial animosities had been obliterated and equality of sexes had been established.

An Indian patriot Mahmud secretly journeyed to Baku on the Caspian via Iran in 1928. In his report to the Soviet authorities he asked them to facilitate these secret visits by Indians and sought support in this endeavour by the Soviet diplomatic staff posted in the country.[5]

In 1930s Indians used the route via Iran and Baku to reah Moscow rather than the old Kabul-Tahkent –Moscow route. When Rahulji went to Leningrad in 1937, he travelled via Iran and Baku. He received help from the Soviet diplomatic staff who had been instructed by their government to aid revolutionaries hailing from European colonies in Asia and Africa. There was one exception. Raja Mahendra Pratap who had been using Kabul-Tashkent route since 1916, succeded in getting Soviet permission to journey through Central Asia in 1930.

Raja Mahendra Pratap had formed the Provisional Government of India in exile in Kabul in 1915.[6] He sent emissaries to the Tsarist Governor of Central Asia and persisted in his efforts to obtain support for his cause when Bolshevik rule replaced the Tsars.[7] When the Bolsheviks closed the Central Asian route for the Indians in mid-1920s, he still insisted on using it. He was flown aboard a Soviet plane to Kabul and in January 1930 was allowed to pass through Tashkent on way to Germany.[8]

The Soviet authorities however subjected Mahendra Pratap to a thorough search and even though he had Soviet permission, they confiscated fifty-five gold roubles he was carrying. On reaching Germany Mahendra Pratap lodged a complain with the Soviet officials.[9]

At the back of the Soviet mind was the desire not to irritate the British rulers of India with whom they had established diplomatic relations after the Anglo-Soviet Trade Agreement of March 1921.[10]

The British government was vigilant that the Soviets provided no overt help to Indian freedom fighters. It had declared that any such help would be construed as a contravention of treaty obligations on the part of the Soviets. In face of British protests, prudence dictated that the Soviets should outwardly do nothing to irritate the British authorities in India. One way to earn British gratitude or approbation was to deny entry to Indians into the Central Asian territories.

Despite this constraint the Soviets were still keen that the subjects of European colonies in Asia and Africa should be acquainted with their achievements in the Central Asian region.

They sponsored visits by Communist Party leaders of colonies to Central Asia. These visitors were taken to collective and co-operative farms where peasant and workers greeted them and recounted to them the beneficial changes that had occurred in their lives in the post-revolutionary era. They showed to the guests that people were better fed and clothed; their children received education. Now they had access to higher education and medical facilities.

An Indian Communist Saklatvala was able to avail this opportunity. Though an Indian, he had settled down in Great Britain and had been twice elected to the House of Commons. Technically he was a member of the British Communist Party.[11]

At this point it should be remembered that the Communist Party of the Great Britain had been authorized by the Comintern to look after the affairs of the Indian Communist Party and this was probably a ploy to convince Indians that Central Asia was not totally barred to them.

During his visit to Central Asia he was taken to a number of places; he spoke at gatherings of workers and peasants. He was deeply impressed by the changes that had occurred in the lives of the common man. He expressed his feelings to his comrade Harry Pollitt, another leader of the Communist Party of Great Britain thus. "Oh Harry , what my people could do in India if only they were as free as my comrades in those autonomous republics in the USSR."[12] The experience gave him renewed energy to fight against British imperialism.[13]

For social and political activists, the socio-economic and cultural transformation achieved in the Central Asian Republics was a matter of wonder and great admiration.

Rahul Sankrityayan, a member of the Communist Party of India was an eminent scholar of Buddhism and Tibetan history. He was greatly attracted to Central Asia. He wanted to visit the ancient Buddhist sites in Central Asia to satisfy his intellectual curiosity and also to see the changes that had been brought about in the country by communism. He thought Central Asia could act as a model for social engineering in India. He had already published a book on Marxism, *Samyavad hi Kyon* (in Hindi) and wanted to see how communism operated in practice.

During his visit to Japan in 1935, he managed to get a transit visa via Moscow, Baku and Iran to travel to India. His efforts to get Soviet permission to spend five weeks in the country and visit Leningrad, Moscow, Baku, Samarkand and Tajikistan and to return to India via Afghanistan was turned down.[14]

In 1937 Rahulji was invited by the famous Soviet Buddhist scholar Prof Schcherbatsky to collaborate with him on the preparation of an authentic text of *Vritialankara.* Rahulji took this opportunity and travelled to Leningrad via Iran. He continued to read and discuss the developments in Soviet Central Asia. His studies convinced him that remarkable changes had taken place there.[15] He collected material so that he could write a book on the Soviet Union. He sought permission to visit Central Asia but did not succeed.[16] However he got a chance to spend four days in Central Asia while returning to India via Afghanistan in January 1938. He was allowed to board a train leaving Moscow for Stalinabad (Dushambe), the capital of Tajikistan. Leaving Moscow on 15 January 1938, he reached Termez on 21 January,[17] a town situated on the banks of the Oxus river in Uzbekistan. On the other side of the Oxus lay Afghanistan.

The brief stay of four days in Termez was Rahulji's first and last first hand experience of life in Soviet Central Asia. All his subsequent efforts to go to Central Asia for collecting data for a book on Central Asia failed.

Since his visit to Termez was not sponsored, Rahulji was free to go wherever he liked and could meet persons of his own choice.

He went to a school and was deeply impressed by the questions put to him about India by the young boys and girls.[18]

He then visited a nearby village and saw a collective farm where tractors and other machines were used in farming.[19] What impressed him most was that none of farmers was shabbily clothed or looked ill-nourished or unhappy.[20]

Next day he traveled to another village, established only ten years ago after a canal was dug out of the Oxus river. The farm was spread over one thousand acres of land and had a tractor and two lorries. The village had a school where 35 girls and 53 boys were studying. The classes started at eight in the morning and continued up to six in the evening with a break of two hours from 12 to 2 P.M.[21] The school had two teachers and the medium of instruction was Uzbek language. Latin script had now replaced the Arabic script for the Uzbek language.[22] He was happy to see that rural poverty endemic in India was completely absent in Soviet Central Asia.

Rahulji received all courtesies from the local population with whom he came in contact. The Uzbek teacher introduced to him his wife, who was a Russian. Rahulji remarked that such mixed marriages between Europeans and Asians were becoming quite common. He hoped that by the end of the century racial distinctions in social relationship would cease to exist.[23] Rahulji could not visualize that in the next half a century the Soviet Union would disintegrate and Central Asians would be masters of their own fate.

Rahulji also commented on the cultural progress made since the revolution. The village Club was its symbol. It had five rooms along with a Hall with a seating capacity of 500.The Hall was used for screening films, shown by a travelling cine-unit which came to village once in a while.[24]

The Club also had a library stocked with current newspapers. The villagers were informed about things happening in the country and the world.[25]

The state was taking good care of the cultural requirements of the population.

Rahulji observed the manner in which the agricultural operations were carried out. Different groups consisting of men and women called *brigad* were formed and each *brigad* was assigned a specific tasks. A chief coordinated the activities of all the *brigads.*[26]

When agricultural operations started, the workers organized a *creche* managed by village women. Rahulji was happy that infants were well cared for when their mothers were engaged in farming.[27]

The village concentrated upon producing Egyptian cotton although some farmers cultivated vegetables. Farmers grew fruit trees on their private patch.

Rahulji found out that last year the farm had earned eight hundred thousand roubles (about four lakh rupees) by the sale of cotton.[28] It was clear that the income was good and the peasant was economically well off now.

During his visit to the village he also met a group of five cyclists from Termez of whom one was Russian and the rest were Uzbeks. All of them were good friends and there was no trace of racial animosity.[29] Rahulji was convinced that under new dispensation racism had been wiped out.

On way back to Termez a local person befriended Rahulji. He soon became very fond of him. While passing by a blue dome- topped mosque, his friend informed him that it was being repaired by the Archaeological Department of the Government. In course of conversation he was told that before the revolution the mosque was a centre of pilgrimage and devotees came here from far and near to pray for the fulfillment of their wishes. They also offered gifts to the shrine. Now hardly anyone came to pray. The youngsters did not believe in organized religion. This made Rahulji extremely happy. As a Marxist he considered religion to be a baneful effect on society and regarded it as a great obstruction in the path of social transformation. Socialism had succeeded in banishing religion even from the highly conservative Muslim societies.[30]

Rahulji was also told that a few years back some Muslims observed fast during the holy month of Ramzan. But now they had given up this practice. Organised religion had lost its hold even over the rural population. The news was very gratifying to Rahulji, who thought the same could now be successfully practised India where people were religious minded. For Rahulji this was another proof that Marxism had the power to usher in radical changes in people's attitude, surmounting centuries-old beliefs, traditions and practices.

Rahulji also noticed great improvements made in the status of women. Muslim women had come out of the four-walls of houses and were walking on the road unveiled. It seemed socialism had established gender equality even in Muslim societies. He found the same thing on the banks of the Oxus river where Russian and local women were working together. The empowerment of Muslim women was a sure sign of social transformation brought about by the Bolsheviks.[31] Rahulji witnessed gender equality while visiting the Club as well. He found men and women writing posters announcing the screening of a new film in the coming weeks.[32]

Racial equality ensured by socialism was evident when he found a drunk Russian and an Uzbek dancing together in the street. He marked the absence of racism when he found a mixed crew on the boat taking him to the opposite bank. The workers included Russians and Uzbeks; they were eating together.[33]

Rahulji during his short visit of four days to Termez was convinced that socialism had great power for social, economic and cultural transformation. In a brief span of time it had thrown out the "capitalists, the God and the Priest"to Afghanistan, to the other side of the river.[34]

The visit left a deep impression on the mind of Rahulji. He realised that political activism was the need of the hour in India. He plunged into active politics, led peasant revolts and participated in movements against the British government. The colonial masters of India sent him to prison for defying the established authority.

The scholar in Rahulji was also aroused. He now determined to write a fully researched history of Central Asia and also to acquaint his compatriots with the benign consequences of the Soviet rule. He was keen that he should spend a longer period in the Central Asian region to collect data for his proposed work. He intended to study in local libraries and archives and to visit ancient monuments and sites of archaeological excavations carried on by the Soviet scholars.

In 1944 when Rahulji was planning to visit the Soviet Union he wrote to the Soviet government to grant him permission to enter Central Asia. In March 1944, before he left for Moscow via Iran, he wrote to Prof Kalyanov, a Sanskritist, who was then working at the Institute of Oriental Studies, Tashkent to intercede on his behalf with the Soviet authorities.[35]

In March 1946, after having spent about eighteen months in Leningrad, Rahulji wrote to the Soviet authorities to permit him to spend the period between 15 March and 15 October in Central

Asia. His application was forwarded to the Deputy Minister of Foreign Affairs, USSR. Rahuli wrote a personal letter to the Foreign Minister, USSR, telling him of his desire 'to write a book "Soviet Central Asia" in three volumes, depicting the people, their history and their achievements in economic, social and cultural spheres through the ages. He wanted to visit Central Asia 'in order to collect necessary materials... and to cover all the five republics, Turkmenia, Tajkistan, Uzbekistan, Kirgizia and Kazakhstan.'[36]

He did not receive any reply. In sheer desperation on 30 September 1946, Rahulji addressed a letter to Comrade Stalin, the General Secretary of the Communist Party of the Soviet Union and the final decision-making authority, informing him that he had been 'entrusted' (sic) by the "Indian Communist Party to write a book about Soviet Central Asia (the five republics of Kazakhstan, Kirghiziya, Uzbekistan, Turkmenia and Tadjikstan) showing how the Soviet Power [Communismus (sic)] solved the problems and transformed the Tsarist colonial slaves into the free, prosperous and cultured soviet republics. Such a book will serve very useful purpose as there are close similarities between the present politico-economic and socio-religious problems of India and those of pre-revolutionary Central Asia."[37]

He also furnished a synopsis of the proposed book planned in three volumes. 'The first volume is to deal with the historical development of Central Asian nationalities, their strife and sufferings from primitive life to the Tsarist exploitation and final liberation and achievements under Leninist-Stalinist guidanc(sic). Much of the material parts of the book are the Volume II and III intended to give the clear picture of the life of the people, the life in all asupects (sic), the countryside covered with the blooming kolkhozes and sovkhozes (sic), their cities full of the factories (sic) and industrial enterprises, their canals, mines hydroelectric stations, their cultural achievements educational institutions univesitis (sic) and academies.'

He went on to add, "My purpose would have been served by the visit of the selected places with an official gude (sic). I could gather much of the materials for writing and illustration in the cities like Ashkabad, Stalinabad, Leningrad, Bokhara, Samarkand, Tashkend, Frunze, Jambul, Alma-Ata, Karganda and villages nearby."[38]

Rahulji again pointed out that the Indian Communist Party had in their letter in June 1946 asked him to write the book on Central Asia and fulfill his mission.[39]

On 4 October 1946, M.A. Suslov on behalf of Stalin conveyed to Zhadanov that 'the academic tour/field trip of Rahul Sankrityayan to the Soviet Central Asian Republics was not advisable.'[40]

Rahulji did not lose hope. He continued to press for permission for an academic trip to the Soviet Central Asia. In June 1946, Kozlov wrote to the Deputy to the Head of the Department of Foreign Policy regarding Rahulji's proposal. He briefly mentioned Rahulji's Communist background stating that he was 'a member of the Communist Party of India and former leader of the All India Peasant Organization…'. Rahulji had stated that ' before he came to the USSR the leaders of the Central Committee of Communist Party of India directed him to study the situation in the USSR and especially one of the Central Asian Republics so that after his return Sankrityayan may write a large volume on the USSR, which would be published by the Central Committee of the Communist Party of India in various Indian languages.'[41]

The letter went on to add, "… during his stay in Leningrad Sanrityayan translated a large volume on Soviet Tajikistan by a Tajik writer and himself wrote a book on the USSR."

Kozlov further wrote," Considering the growth of interest about the USSR in India especially at present as well as the fact that that Rahul Sankrityayan in 1938 itself published a book on the USSR named "Soviet Bhumika" (sic) (Soviet Land) in India, for which he was subjected to persecution by the by the (sic) British Government, whereas his new publications will draw the attention of broad group of Indian readers."

He then concluded, "It is advisable to invite Sankrityayan… (illegible)".

The Soviet government did not change its decision; Rahulji

never got a chance to travel to Central Asia .[42] He survived for another decade and a half and wrote a book *Soviet Madhya Asia* in Hindi and published *Madhya Asiya ka Itihas* in Hindi in two volumes in early 1950s. For this he was awarded the Sahitya Akademi Prize. To this day this work remains the most comprehensive history of Central Asia published in Hindi. Rahulji had put in all his scholarship in these volumes, now renowned as a literary piece as well.

Rahulji's inability to go on a field trip to Central Asia was the result of a deliberate decision taken by the Soviet authorities at the highest level. We do not know what prompted them to do this. If they wanted to keep away foreigners from going to the Soviet Central Asia, they hardly succeeded. Events in the world politics were moving at a fast pace and they could not keep the wheel of History from rolling.

The Second World War broke out in Europe and USSR became an ally of Nazi Germany.

In India patriots started dreaming of using this opportunity to enlist German support against the British rule to win their independence as they had done during the First World War. Netaji Subhas Chandra Bose secretly left Calcutta where he was under house arrest and arrived in Kabul on 27 January 1941. Immediately he contacted both the German and the Soviet missions. He sought asylum in the Soviet Union. But the Soviet government turned down his request. It did not want to antagonize the British rulers of India. Bose then turned to the German Embassy. The German Foreign Office agreed to his request and permitted him to come to Berlin. The problem was he had to pass through the Soviet territory. The Soviet authorities were unwilling to concede even this respect. However after much persuasion by the Axis Powers they consented to his arrival in the Soviet Union in disguise but did not permit him to stay in the Soviet Union. The Italian Embassy issued a Passport to Bose in the name of Orlando Mazzorotto and Bose traveled to Berlin under this name. The Soviets kept his journey to Berlin via Moscow a top secret. He was, however never given a chance to visit Central Asia or interact with the local population.

This incident shows the attitude of the Soviet government towards Indian freedom fighters. National interests gained precedence over ideological preferences.

The Soviet policy of discouraging or banning Indians to the Soviet Central Asia persisted in the early years after the Second World War ended, as is shown by their denial of permission to Rahulji to conduct academic field-work in Soviet Central Asia.[43]

The Soviet-German alliance did not last. Hitler launched an attack on the Soviet Union in June 1941. The German forces met with initial success. They besieged Leningrad and were within striking distance of Moscow. The Soviets asked all academic institutions to evacuate Leningrad and Moscow. The Institute of Oriental Studies of the Academy of Sciences USSR was relocated in Tashkent. Senior scholars who could not be sent to the front were asked to move to Tashkent and to carry on their work there. The Institute was attached to USFAN (Uzbek Branch of the USSR Academy of Sciences).[44]

Among scholars of Indian studies who arrived in Tashkent were two Indians. We learn about them from the memoirs of Prof Koka Aleksandrovna Antonova who was also among the team of Soviet Indian scholars in Tashkent. At this point of time she is unable to recall their names although she remembers their nick-names, Lopez and Litton. The former, Lopez, was a middle-aged Sikh and may have been one of those Ghadar Party inmates who had been sent to Moscow by the Ghadar Party from USA in 1930s.The other, Litton, was a Bengali who was not well-educated and gave lessons in spoken Bengali. He eventually succeeded in securing a Kandidat's degree and after the war shifted to Moscow. For sometime he was a teacher of Bengali language in Moscow State University. He was an indifferent teacher. He left Moscow for some other city in the USSR. (Information given to the author in June 1999 in Moscow by Dr E.N. Komarov, a Faculty Member of Indian Sector of the Institute Of Oriental Studies, Academy of Sciences, Russia. Dr Komarov studied Bengali with him at the Moscow State University after the Second World War ended.)

We have no idea what these two Indians did at the Institute. My guess is that along with helping Russian scholars Dyakov,

Reusner and Balabushevich in their researches on India, they also worked at the Radio Tashkent which had begun its broadcast in Indian languages.

A Russian document reveals that two Indians (names unknown) lived in Tajikistan. They were planning to cross into India secretly and to stir trouble against the British rule. The Soviet government insisted that this should be done in strict secrecy and not a word should be uttered about the involvement of the Soviet government. We have no idea if they ever made this trip.

Conclusion: It is clear that from mid-1920s the Soviets had decided not to allow Indians to use Central Asian territories as a base for their operation against the British rule in India. They discouraged Indians from coming to Central Asia. Indians who were keen to go to the USSR now traveled via Iran and Baku, bypassing Soviet Central Asia. Once in a while the Soviet authorities did deviate from this practice but Indians passing through Central Asia were exceptions rather than rule. However, for Indians Central Asia was a symbol, a symbol of absence of racism, freedom from capitalist exploitation, modernization and social transformation. Hence Soviet Central Asia was repeatedly invoked in their fight against British colonialism, religious obscurantism and gender discrimination.

Footnotes

1. Surendra Gopal (ed.), *India and Central Asia,* Delhi,2001, pp. 99-138
2. See my brochure *Indian Freedom-Fighters In Tashkent:1917-1922 Contesting Ideologies: Nationalism, Pan Islamism and Marxism*, Kolkata, 2002 and its revised version *Supra.*
3. Zagorodnikova and Shastitko (chief editors), *Russko-Indiiskiye Otnosheniya v 1900 -1917 gg.,* Moskva,1999, Docs no. 323-342. The documents reproduce the correspondence between Barkatullah, Mahendra Pratap and Tsarist and Bolshevik officials between 12 February 1916 and 29 November 1919
4. Markowits,pp. 105-06
5. Roy, Datta Gupta and Vasudevan (eds), *Indo- Russian Relations* 1917-1947,Part I 1917-1928 (henceforth cited as Indo-Russian

Relations I),Calcutta, 1999,pp.35459,doc. No.135

6. *Indo-Russian Relations I,* pp. 1-4
7. Ibid.,pp.56-57, Doc no. 27; Ibid., pp. 149-58, Doc. No. 56
8. Roy, Datta Gupta and Vasudevan (eds), *Indo-Russian Relations 1917-47, Part II,*1929-47 (henceforth cited as *Indo-Russian Relations II*), Calcutta, 2000, pp 363-3
9. *Indo-Russian Relations II*, pp. 368-69, Doc. Nos. 106 and 107
10. C.S.Samra, *India and Anglo-Soviet Relations* (1917-1947), New Delhi,1959,p. 56
11. Panchanan Saha, *Shapurji Saklatvala,* New Delhi, 1970, p. 60
12. Ibid., p. 61
13. Ibid.
14. *Indo- Russian Relations II* ,pp. 388-89
15. Aruna Haldar, "Lonely, Majestic Sojourner," *The Times Of India,* Patna, 12 July 1993
16. Rahulji collected more material during his stay in Leningrad in 1945-47 and was able to publish in two volumes a history of Central Asia in Hindi. Rahul Sankrityayan, *Madhya Asiya ka Itihas* (in Hindi) ,Part I, Patna, 1956, p. *gha*
17. Rahul Sankrityayan, *Meri Jeevan Yatra* (in Hindi) ,Volume II, Allahabad,1950, pp. 460-64
18. Ibid., pp.46-67
19. Ibid., p. 467
20. Ibid.
21. Ibid., p. 468
22. Ibid.
23. Ibid.
24. Ibid., pp. 468-469
25. Ibid, p. 468
26. Ibid., p. 469
27. Ibid.
28. Ibid.
29. Ibid.
30. Ibid., p. 469-70
31. Ibid., p. 470
32. Ibid.
33. Ibid., pp. 470-71
34. Ibid., p.470
35. *Indo-Russian Relations II*, p.390
36. Ibid., pp. 390-92
37. Ibid., pp. 393-394

38. Ibid. ,p. 395
39. Ibid.
40. Ibid, p. 396
41. Ibid. ,pp. 396-97
42. Ibid. ,p. 397
43. H.N.Pandit, *Netaji Subhas Chandra Bose From Kabul to Battle of Imphal* (Sterling Publishers Private Limited, Delhi), pp.1-6
44. K.A. Antonova, "Recollection of Personal Encounters With Indians In The USSR In 1930s-1940s", *The Social Engineer*, Vol.9, No. 1, January 2000, pp.140-42.

Intellectual Encounters

Central Asians and Indian Studies 1950s to 1991

Since the early nineteenth century a bunch of Russian scholars mostly based in Moscow and St. Petersburg (Leningrad) were engaged in studies on Indian history, society and culture; their efforts were mostly confined to the classical period; they were primarily concerned with religion, philosophy, Sanskrit and Pali languages and the story of Russo-Indian contacts. Russian scholars widened their areas of concern in course of the century which also saw increasing Russo-English colonial rivalry over Central Asia and India.

The Tsarist administration feared British penetration in the region while the English thought that Russian advance could endanger the safety of their possessions in India. The Russians kept their army prepared for a possible attack by the British on Central Asia. First they established a listening post in Ashkabad, but soon switched on to Tashkent and made it a valuable window to happenings in India and Afghanistan. Tashkent-based military officers keenly followed the events in India till the October Revolution replaced the Tsarist regime by Soviet rule. The object was purely utilitarian: to gather and disseminate information useful to Russians for political and military purposes. They conducted their studies in Russian and shunned local languages. As a part of this strategy, they initiated a programme to teach Indian languages, especially Urdu (Hindustani) to Russian army officers.

Indian studies were started to cater to Russian military needs.

In 1895 a proposal was put forward [1] to teach Hindustani properly to army officers. So far Indians located in Tashkent and Bukhara who could teach only conversational Urdu were employed; they had no idea of grammar and other nuances of the language. Military needs prompted Russians to begin the teaching of modern Indian languages in Central Asia. Sanskrit did not form the core of Indian studies as was the case of European countries. Here the trajectory of Indian studies from the very beginning was different. In 1896 Lt. A. I. Vyogornitskii was sent to India for an year to update his knowledge of Hindustani. On return he insisted that a teacher must be brought from India in order to give proper training to Russian officers in Hindustani.

Vyogornitskii diligently set about his task. In 1898 he published from Tashkent a textbook for the study of Hindustani or Urdu and appended to it a Russian-Hindustani dictionary useful for military purposes.[2] To him goes the credit of starting the teaching of modern Indian languages in Central Asia.

Grulev's writings in local newspapers showed enhanced Russian interest in India; they paid more attention to current events, especially on the North- western borders of India since these were of immediate interest to Tashkent on account of geographical proximity. Grulev discussed Anglo-Russian concerns on the Indian north- western frontiers[3] where the two powers were standing face to face. He wrote about the problem of Chitral[4] and Baluchistan[5]—an area of deep strategic concern to the British at the turn of the twentieth century. In 1905 and 1906 Yagello also published three articles on Baluchistan.[6].

I.P. Yagello was an army officer who had returned from Paris after studying Urdu. Lt. Col. Yagello commenced teaching Hindustani at Ashkhabad but soon went to Tashkent to teach Hindustani.[7] He was simultaneously the Secretary of the Tashkent branch of Russian Oriental Society, formed in 1900 by the Russian Government under a Decree signed by Vitte, the Russian Finance Minister.[8] Tsar Nicholas II approved its constitution in 1910.(Information supplied by Prof. L.B. Alayev.)

It was a clear signal that Tsarist circles had decided to promote oriental studies in a systematic manner in order to provide inputs to their foreign policies and military planning. The spurt in the publication of articles in Tashkent press and close attention given to the teaching of Indian languages should be seen against this background.

Yagello published a grammar of Urdu in 1902. He also

brought out a Urdu-Russian Dictionary [9] and other works for improving the instruction of Urdu to Russian army officers.

It was he who prevailed over Russian authorities to bring from India Haji Riazuddin Ahmed, a teacher of Urdu (Hindustani) in 1903[10]. The Indian was well versed in Persian and English. Riazuddin, the first fully qualified teacher, taught Hindustani at Tashkent for three years. His teaching was greatly appreciated. He was awarded a medal for his distinguished services. He was, however, not reemployed at the expiry of his term although he had sought reemployment. Russians had by now a lurking fear that he was a spy of the British government.

By the first decade of the twentieth century Tashkent had emerged as a centre for the study of two major Indian languages, Hindi and Urdu. Local newspapers and journals published articles on happenings in India whenever they seemed to be of military and strategic significance to Russians. The local Press was instrumental in strengthening Indian studies in Central Asia.

The dominant military angle comes through in articles published by Grulev on rail-lines being constructed on the borders of India.[11] The same author discussed Indian rail lines and the question of their link-up with a projected rail line of China.[12] Russsia feared a hostile Anglo-Chinese tie up.

Snesaryev dealt with the problem of rail lines in Kashmir.[13]

Yagello also took keen interest in happenings in India .He devoted two articles to Indian trading ties with Persia.[14] He also wrote on Indian trade in 1905-06.

Grulev discussed Anglo- Russian relations on the north-western frontiers of India[15] because it was here that both the powers stood face to face. The same author wrote about the problems of Chitral[16] and Baluchistan,[17] of deep concern to colonial master of India at the turn of the last century. In 1905 and 1906 Yagello published three more articles on Baluchistan.[18]

Another specialist on Indian affairs who came into lime-light was Losyev. He wrote on Indian commerce with western Tibet because after Col. Younghusband's invasion of Tibet, the Tibetan question was in the fore-front of Anglo-Chinese relations.[19] Russia's attempt to woo Dalai Lama during the past two decades had failed.

It is clear that more attention was paid to the study of events taking place on the North-western borders of India since these developments were of immediate interest to Tsarist authorities in Tashkent as they feared their adverse impact on defenses of Russian-held Central Asia. Earlier in 1898 and 1899 Grulev penned a series of articles on the situation in the north-western frontier of India, particularly in the tribal belt where uprisings had taken place and the British had adopted ruthless measures to suppress them. The idea was to give Russian readers a continuing military appraisal of this sensitive border area.[20]

Grulev and Yagello also wrote several articles in the closing years of the nineteenth and the opening decade of the twentieth century on political conditions in British India. There is an article on the Indian National Congress, the premier political organization of Indians;[21] there are articles and notes on the position of the Muslims[22] and the Revolutionary movement in the country.[23] The Muslims had started maintaining a distance from the Indian National Congress and were organizing themselves separately. This was also the time when some Indian youths had taken up the 'cult of bomb' to free their motherland from alien domination.

Grulev, Yagello and Losyev, the three chief commentators on Indian affairs in the Tashkent press at the close of the nineteenth and the opening of the twentieth century, were all highly placed military officers. Their studies on India were exclusively concerned with contemporary political and military events. They were meant to provide inputs for Russian policy framers with regard to the defence of Russian Central Asia. The only exceptions seem to have been biographies of Akbar and Nadir Shah.[24] The teaching of Hindustani and the regular publication of articles on India had created a congenial atmosphere for the development of Indian studies in Tashkent.

When the Soviets came to power after the November Revolution of 1917, they could not overlook Tashkent's pivotal place in tracking the course of events in India. In the light of knowledge so far gained, the Soviets could develop their attitudes towards European colonies, especially India in the context of their anti-imperial, anti-colonial and anti-racial ideology. This entailed a shift in the focus of Indian studies; they ceased to be the preserve of the bureaucratic-military establishment though they remained tied to the apron strings of the government.

Post-November 1917 Revolution: A New Stage In Indian Studies

The Soviet state, born after the November Revolution of 1917, proclaimed itself as a promoter of world-revolution against anti-colonialism and imperialism. The Communist International or Comintern was organized to give impetus to the movement. One of the active participants in the Bolshevik Revolution Mikhail Pavlovich (Weltman) (1871-1927) connected with the Ministry of Nationalities and himself greatly interested in contemporary Indian history(he published an article on Mahatma Gandhi) formed the Vsesouuznaya Nauchnaya Assostsiatsia Vostokovedeniya (VNAV) in 1921 to promote oriental studies in the country. This organization was attached to the Central Committee of Communist Party and therefore, commanded attention It laid policy guidelines for oriental scholars.[25] It criticized the traditional Russian oriental studies and dubbed them as 'bourgeois'. Traditional oriental scholars were simply tolerated.

Pavlovich also brought out a Journal, '*Novyi Vostok*' (New East) which published the researches of the newly established school of Soviet oriental scholars.

The State in the new dispensation sponsored oriental studies; it set the parameters within which scholars were required to function. The Society had a brief existence. Once Stalin decided on the policy of 'revolution in one country', the Soviet State became lukewarm to the growth of oriental studies. Pavlovich died in 1927 and the Association died with him.[26] It seems that the Government policy was initially to promote the study of modern oriental languages. They were creating a Soviet cadre for propagating their ideology in colonies. India was prime target since freedom movement was gaining momentum within the country and the British government was engaged in suppressing it. In pursuit of this objective the Russian Oriental Society established Oriental Language Institute in November 1918 at Tashkent for imparting teaching in Sanskrit and Urdu languages.[27]

S.F. Oldenberg, the famous Buddhist scholar was associated with this project. Its teachers mostly came from Russia. After a while some locals also joined the teaching staff.[28]

History was repeating itself. A decade and half earlier Tashkent became a centre for teaching Indian languages to Russian military officers. The perspective had changed; now knowledge and expertise in Indian language was needed for preparing scholars and /or propagators of Marxist ideology. For practical reasons as well the Soviet step was justified.

This was the period when Indian revolutionaries had gathered in Tashkent in substantial numbers. Indian patriots and the Soviets intended to develop Tashkent as a base for conducting anti-British campaign to drive them out of India. The Soviets opened a Military School to train Indians in use of modern weaponry. For a variety of reasons the School had a brief life; it was closed in 1921. The Soviets gave up their plans about converting Tashkent into a military base; they asked Indian patriots to move to Moscow. The city had in a brief period carved out for itself a permanent place in the history of Indian freedom struggle.

In early 1920, with so many Indians around and a lot more expected to join them, the local press, both the Russian and Uzbek press showed keen interest in the happenings in India. They regularly published news about India; they also focused on activities of Indians in Tashkent.[29]

Some academic research on India was carried out. These were mostly published in Russian language This was a new dimension of Indian studies in Tashkent. At the same time some researchers brought out in Uzbek language publications of a popular nature to satisfy the curiosity of the common man. Maliev's, history of India in Uzbek language, published in Tashkent in 1920 was probably the most significant work of this genre.[30] It was probably the first complete history of India written in Uzbek language.

The change in Soviet policy towards Indian freedom fighters in Tashkent did not result in stoppage of Indian studies; they were to satisfy academic curiosity and serve a utilitarian purpose for a government committed to usher in a world proletarian revolution. Colonial India, a nation of 300 million, the second largest in the world, deserved prompt attention.

Government patronage to Indian studies continued. In 1924, the above-mentioned Oriental Language Institute was made an independent Faculty and was taken over by the Tashkent University. Indian studies in Central Asia became a part of the University system and a component of higher studies.

This did not last long. The Faculty was closed towards the end of 1920s when the Soviets by the end of 1920s decided to concentrate on economic development and their interest in sustaining Indian studies waned.

Indian Studies were revived in Tashkent only during the Second World War; in the interregnum the local press off and on covered Indian affairs.

Henceforth the Tashkent press primarily highlighted events connected with the freedom movement in India since the Soviets had proclaimed support for colonial peoples fighting against their imperial rulers. The obsession with military affairs of the pre-revolutionary era was gone; the press was full of reports on labour movement, mass agitations and events, showing the colonial rule in a bad light.

However there was a positive fall out for Soviet indology. Interaction with Indians in early 1920s in Tashkent contributed indirectly to the promotion of Indian studies in the Soviet Union. Several future Russian indologists developed interest in Indian studies owing to their contacts with Indians in Central Asia during this period.

Prominent among such persons were A.M. Dyakov, one time a Minister of Health and a medicine man by education. He wrote widely on medieval, modern periods of Indian history, and during his life time was one of the senior- most experts on India in the Soviet Union.

Another doctor, B.L. Smirnov, developed a liking for Sanskrit and devoted his spare time to translating the Mahabharata in verse into Russian. He remained at Ashkhabad, capital of the Republic of Turkmenistan.

Goldberg, a Soviet Indologist of the same era began his career as a liaison officer with the Indians at Tashkent.[31] He was the member of the Board of Chief Editors for two major volumes on India, *Russko-Indiiskiye Otnosheniya v XVII v.* (Moscow, 1958) and *Russko-Indiiskiye Otnosheniya v XVIII v.* (Moscow, 1965). These works were subsequently followed by two more volumes of documents on Russo-Indian Relations; one dealt with the XIX Century and the other with the period from 1900 to 1917.

The obsession with military affairs of the pre-revolutionary era was gone. The Bolsheviks now set the terms for Central Asian intellectual encounter with India. The Soviet concepts of international proletarian revolution and anti-colonialism, anti-capitalism supplied the ideological underpinnings of the new encounter.

Indian Studies in the Inter-war Period

The ideological slant in newspaper reports and articles and journals was inevitable because the Soviets planned to show to the people of Tashkent how communism had effectively made them a progressive modern nation while other European Asian colonies were still languishing in servitude, educational backwardness and grinding poverty.

When the Simon Commission from England visited India to recommend measures for constitutional progress, Indians boycotted it and *en masse* showed their displeasure. The Tashkent press informed the readers about the deep resentment it had stirred up along with the repressive steps of the government.[32]

The *Byuletin* also published material on Indian railways, labour movement, movement for emancipation of women, the state of Indian native states and the competition for Indian oil between American and British capitalists. [33] Any event smacking of anti-colonial struggle received attention in the local press. The *Byuletin* remained the main source in Tashkent for disseminating information about India till 1931 when the mantle fell upon *Na Zarubezhnom Vostoke.*

In early thirties the tribal belt in the north-western frontier of India was in ferment. The Red Shirt Movement launched by

Khan Abdul Ghaffar Khan directed against the colonial masters was gaining momentum. The British adopted repressive measures. The Tashkent press took notice of it.[34] When the Pathans took to arms in retaliation, articles highlighting the defiance of the Pathans were printed.[35] Some of these informative articles were translations from British journals.[36] The Press did take note of mass movements that emerged in India during this period. The uprisings in Kashmir and Alwar against the local Maharajas were reported.[37]

After the November Revolution, the Soviet scholars on India pursued with deep interest the course of labour and peasant movements. In 1932 an article on the above topic was printed.[38] Another article in 1934 based on foreign press reports described the condition of the workers and the "state of their movement."[39] The author, Reusner, was one of the foremost experts on India in the then Soviet Union.

The state of Indian agriculture was an object of special study. *Na Zarubezham Vostoke* (No. 2, 1932) published a note on Indian agriculture. U. Roslavlev published two long articles in the same journal in the issues of 1933 and 1934 about the development of landlordism and the agrarian plicy of British Imperialists in India. Prof. Reusner, whose students formed the nucleus of Soviet specialists on India in the Post-world war II period, contributed a brilliant analytical paper on "Agrarian Crisis and Peasant's Movement in India in 1933" to *Revolution and Culture in Central Asia* (a collection of papers, Tashkent, 1934). These articles put all blame for the backwardness of Indian agriculture at the door of the British, the colonial masters of India..

In 1930s as war clouds appeared on the horizon, Tashkent press took note of events of military significance.

Tashkent also continued its role of being the Soviet Union's observation post for watching events of military importance in India. Anything even remotely affecting the security of the country was taken note of. In 1928, when projects for strengthening the English air might were on the anvil, the Tashkent press denounced the step as an Imperialist plot and as a preparation for a future war.[40] The local press continued to criticize the measures adopted by the English to improve the air force in India in 1929, 1931 and 1934.[41] Articles dealing with Indian army and the state of British preparedness in India also appeared.[42] All the studies with one exception were in Russian.

Tashkent was during this period simply a reporter of Indian events. There was no specialized institution supporting Indian studies; there were no specialists on India. Thus before the Second World War broke out, Tashkent had ceased to be a centre of India studies though its links with India had not been completely snapped. The situation changed dramatically within a short period.

Indian Studies during the Second World War

This was the state of Indian studies when the Second World War broke out. After Hitler attacked the Soviet Union in 1941 pursuit of scholarly activities was almost impossible in European and Caucasian republics. The Soviet government relocated the sector of Indian studies in Tashkent, where there was a not too old tradition of Indian studies and where there was a semblance of infrastructure for the purpose. Several Soviet Indologists staying in Tashkent during these trying years carried on Indian studies. Tashkent, by accident of history, was now the main seat of Indian studies in the Soviet Union though for a brief period. When the war ended in 1945, these Indologists left Tashkent and went back to Moscow and Leningrad.

Indian studies in Tashkent during this small interregnum, were carried on in accordance with the policies of the Soviet government. Among important Soviet Indologists gathered here were I.M. Reusner, Goldberg, Dyakov, Melman, Balabushevich, K.A. Antonova, etc.[43]

The Post-World war II Scenario

World War II ended in a victory of the Allied powers. The Soviets had contributed significantly to the defeat of Nazi Germany. Though devastated, the Soviet Union was full of confidence. It was keen to take on Capitalist Powers in order to assert the superiority of its principles. It wanted to pursue vigorously its mission to wipe out colonialism, imperialism and racialism from the face of the world. After its success against Fascism it had become a role model for colonies, who looked to it for their emancipation. The Capitalist powers did not take long to understand the new role the Soviet Union was contemplating for itself in world politics. The Cold War was unleashed.

The Soviets correctly understood that they had to woo the colonies where national-liberation struggle was flourishing and the mood was overwhelmingly anti-British. The Soviets decided to accumulate detailed knowledge of colonial societies in order to formulate appropriate policies towards them, mostly located in Asia, Africa and Latin America. Oriental Studies received a new push. Tashkent was assigned a vital role to play. By the end of 1950s Oriental Studies were firmly set on the path of revival.

Indian Studies in 1950s

Soviet perception of contemporary international events determined Tashkent's importance.

Tashkent would be presented as a model to the Islamic world and the ex-colonies, as a symbol of efficacy of socialism to act as a powerful engine of socio-economic transformation and modernization. Its geographical proximity to South and Southeast Asia was an added advantage in carrying the message of triumphant socialism. As international air-travel expanded in 1950s, Tashkent, lying at the crossing of routes between Europe and South Asia and Southeast Asia gained in importance.

The Soviets made Tashkent as their base for propagating socialist ideology to South and Southeast Asian region. Its added advantage was availability of some trained personnel in some of the languages, spoken in the region. This explains why Radio Tashkent started broadcasts to India and Pakistan in Urdu as soon as India and Pakistan became independent in 1947. The Soviet policy unraveled itself after the death of Stalin in 1953 and after the ascent of Khrushchev to power in the Soviet Union. The idea to convert Tashkent into a centre of Oriental Studies persisted.

The Soviets started with India for a variety of reasons. Russo-Indian relations had deep roots in history. India's leadership respected socialist ideology and was firmly committed to anti-imperialism and anti-colonialism. It had refused to go whole hog with the USA in international politics and had maintained a neutral posture in the US-USSR Cold War. The Soviets began by wooing India.

The ball was set rolling when the Soviet Prime Minister Malenkov received Dr. Saifuddin Kitchlew, Chairman, All-India Peace Council during his visit to Moscow in July 1954.After the meeting Dr. Kitchlew gave out that Malenkov had told him that he "would welcome an understanding with India…".According to him "Malenkov was seriously interested in meeting Jawaharlal Nehru" and also that he wanted the two countries should "exchange delegations of scientists, artists and writers."[44] Compulsions of international politics had persuaded the Soviets to extend the hands of friendship towards India. The new policy had a positive impact on strengthening Indian studies in the Soviet Union including Central Asia.

The thaw in the Indo-Soviet relations began after Prime Minister Nehru's visit to the Soviet Union and Central Asia in 1955. There was a renewed interest in Indian history, society and culture in the Soviet Union and its constituent Central Asian Republics. The Soviet authorities sustained this surge of interest since they were embarking on an exercise to improve and intensify relationship between the two countries as a part of their national foreign policy, seeking to draw ex-colonies of western nations into their orbit for strengthening their position in the Cold War unleashed by imperialist powers. India, having attained independence after almost a century of bitter struggle against Great Britain, was a welcome partner for demographic, historical and political and a host of other reasons. Indian response was positive since the Prime Minister Jawaharlal Nehru and other influential members of the ruling class swore in the name of socialism and to some extent, felt ideological affinity with the Soviet system.

India also reciprocated the Soviet gesture. Indian Heads of State and Government visited Tashkent at regular intervals. President Rajendra Prasad came to Tashkent in 1960. Next year Nehru was in Tashkent again. Prime Minister Lal Bahadur Shastri went to Tashkent to participate in talks with Pakistan's President Ayub Khan in January 1966. Presidents Zakir Hussain and V. V. Giri also went to Tashkent in 1968 and 1970 respectively. They all saw the manuscript library and emphasized the historic roots of Indo-Central Asian friendship. In 1960s and 1970s Indo-Soviet relations remained cordial and warm.

The tilt towards India meant that the Soviet Union should have a trained batch of experts in Indian studies with ability to provide inputs to the Soviet authorities in their policy formulation. In general it signalled a conscious decision to win over the newly independent nations of the Third World.

The XX Party Congress held in 1956 set its seal on government policy.

The New Policy

Mikoyan made policy revision explicit in his speech before the historic XX Congress of the CPSU convened to officially approve the policy of deStalinisation. He exhorted Soviet scholars of Orient to study its society and economy. This was not an announcement but a directive. The Soviet intentions were clear when a new Director of the Institute of Oriental Studies, Academy Nauk, USSR was appointed. The person was Bobojon G. Gafurov, who had served as Secretary of the Communist Party of the Republic of Tajikistan from 1946 to 1956. He had considerable administrative experience but more importantly than this was the fact that the Party was convinced of his loyalty.[45] According to an author during the Directorship of Gafurov (1956-1977), the intake of postgraduate students rose ten times and the staff of the Institute increased nine times. In 1977 the staff-members numbered 839.[46] Gafurov also ensured that the academic staff was given opportunity to visit the countries, they studied. Every year in 1960s and 1970s, between 120 and 140 scholars of the Institute went abroad. Kotovskii informs us that as the first Soviet scholar of Indian studies he visited India soon after Gafurov took over as Director of the Institute.[47] Gafurov's choice was also dictated by the fact that he was a trained historian, having defended his Candidate's dissertation in 1941 on "History of

Ismaili sects since early XIX century". He had published historical monographs and papers. He knew the importance of oriental history and its use in national policy formulation. He had the necessary credential for heading this organization at such a crucial juncture. Moreover, coming from a Central Asian Republic, it was expected that scholars hailing from former colonies of Europe on Asian, African and Latin American continents might treat him as 'one among themselves' and not 'as belonging to the other'. It was expected that the Third world would not treat him as an 'alien'.

Bobojon Gafurov

Gafurov was an appropriate choice. He energetically set about to accomplish the assigned task. He showed an understanding of the problem and also exhibited great skill in popularizing oriental studies in the Soviet Union during two decades he held that post. As we shall see, he gave a new orientation to Soviet studies on oriental societies in content and style; he broadened its base by coaxing the Central Asian Republics to introduce the subject in institutions of higher studies; he induced them to open an Institute of Oriental Studies under the auspices of the universities or the Academy of Sciences of the respective Republics. Gafurov heralded the era of systematic and sustained study of oriental societies in Soviet Central Asian Republics.

At the outset it was realized that for real advancement in Oriental Studies, scholars were needed with expertise in the language of the country concerned. As a part of this policy, extensive provision of teaching of oriental languages was made.

Gafurov, the newly appointed Director of Institute Of Oriental Studies, Academy of Sciences, USSR, to show his seriousness in implementing the decisions of the XX Party Congress convened a week-long Congress of Soviet Oriental scholars at Tashkent from 4 June 1957 to 11 June 1957. Here the strategy was charted out for strengthening oriental studies. A major decision was to concentrate initially on promotion of the study of Oriental languages so that a Soviet scholar who decided to take up the study of a particular Afro-Asian or Latin American country was proficient in local language and was able to consult primary source material in the language of the concerned country.

Tashkent's choice for the Congress was no accident. It had a tradition of Oriental studies including Indian studies since Tsarist times. In 1920s the Soviets unsuccessfully tried to develop Tashkent as a base for Indian revolutionaries, keen to drive out their colonial masters. During the Second World War, it was the seat of senior Soviet scholars on India, who had been evacuated from Moscow and Leningrad when Nazi forces threatened to overrun these cities. As soon as India became an independent nation, Radio Tashkent had started broadcasts in Urdu language, beamed to India and Pakistan.[48]

Tashkent did possess basic facilities for promoting Indian studies. Once the Soviets were clear in their mind about developing their relations with India, several things started happening at the same time. Some of them had a direct or indirect bearing on the development of Indian studies in Central Asia.

The Soviets needed to expand their embassy staff in Delhi; as a part of the new staffing pattern they decided to induct Hindi and Urdu knowing Soviet citizens. One such person shifted to Delhi was Vladimir Sergeevich Moskalev, the first Head of Hindi and Urdu department of Tashkent Government University and the author of Russian-Urdu Dictionary, published from Tashkent in 1943.[49] He was also the author of *Urdu Language Reader and Urdu-Russian Converstion Book, etc.*[50]

The transfer of Moskalev, created a void; Hardat Madan an Indian from Punjab, gaoled during Stalinist days for entering the Soviet Union without valid papers was released and asked to teach conversational Urdu in the University and help the staff of Radio Tashkent in their broadcasts to India. Even though Hardat was not a trained teacher, he was able to motivate his students and enhance their interest in Indian studies. The Soviets knew that this could only be temporary arrangement and they wanted to find someone with academic credentials for the subject.

Soon they found Haider Yuldashev, who had learnt Hindi and Urdu in pre-war days. He was invited to fill the position created by the departure of Moskalev. He also became the guiding spirit in the Hindi and Urdu broadcasts beamed to India on

Tashkent Radio.[51]

The Soviet Union, to prove its determination to foster Oriental Studies, hosted the XXV International Congress of Orientalists in Moscow in 1960. For the first time Soviet Oriental Scholars *en masse* interacted with their peers from different parts of the world. They learnt about the achievements of their fellow-workers in their field in other parts of the world. Their interest in pursuing oriental studies was heightened.

The Soviet government introduced a course for the study of Indian philology in the Oriental Faculty of Tashkent University under the guidance of V. S. Moskalev and I. D. Serebryanikov. The later had published an article on Rabindranath Tagore in 1955 in the local newspaper *Zvezda Vostoka* (Star of the East) and had continued writing on Indian themes for local newspapers from time to time.[52]

Experts in Indian Languages

The task of having a trained cadre of specialists on India in near future had assumed importance also because Indo-Soviet Co-operation in economic and cultural field was widening day by day.

The Soviets were setting up factories in India and Indians were coming to the Soviet Union for short periods for technical experience. The Soviets needed interpreters with knowledge of Indian languages with the team of Soviet experts both in India and the USSR. The Soviet Information Department both in India and USSR began publishing journals, brochure, etc., in Indian languages. For this they required Indian language specialists. Their need for Soviet citizens knowledgeable in Indian languages, history and society went on increasing as they unleashed a propaganda offensive, trying to project their best image in India through journals, brochures, books, etc. Soviet experts on India were called upon to inform and educate their countrymen about India, now an object of warm Soviet friendship.

Expanding Indo-Soviet contacts also helped to deepen Soviet interest in India. Regular flights, Delhi- Moscow-Delhi and Moscow-Delhi- Moscow, were operating. The planes halted at Tashkent for refueling. Air India staff was stationed at Tashkent.

Indians at Tashkent became a familiar figure from mid-1950s onwards.

Central Asian experts in Indian studies showed the humane face of Soviet rule to India, i.e. the Soviets had shed racial arrogance; the Soviets cared for their backward citizens and had spread total literacy and transformed Central Asia into a modern region. The Soviet claim of brotherhood of all human beings was genuine and not a propaganda gimmick.

The effort to promote Indian studies in Tashkent acquired urgency since Tashkent Radio had started broadcasts to India in Urdu as soon as India became independent in 1947; they needed people proficient in written and spoken Urdu. Initially the shortage was met by recruiting Mr. Haider who had studied Urdu in prewar years in Moscow/ Leningrad and by associating an Indian, a Panjabi, Madan Mohan Hardat, who had come to the Soviet Union in pre-World War II days and had been arrested and put into gaol. Hardat was familiar with both spoken and written Urdu and was a great help in continuing Tashkent Radio broadcasts to India and also in teaching conversational Urdu at the Tashkent University. This, of course, was a temporary arrangement. [53] A multi-dimensional strategy was adopted to prepare a cadre of experts in Indian languages, mainly in Hindi and Urdu, the two most widely –spoken and used languages in India.

Provision was made for teaching Hindi and Urdu in some secondary schools in important cities of Uzbekistan such as Tashkent, Samarkand, Andijan and Namangan. [54]

The Soviet authorities decided to improve the quality of the language of broadcasts beamed to India. They invited people from India to man the staff. In Tashkent the earliest invitee was Habib Saheb, a member of the Indian Communist Party and the son of an important leader, Dr. Syed Mahmud, who was a close friend of the Indian Prime-Minister, Jawaharlal Nehru and also a Congress member of the Ministry in Bihar. Habib was considered trustworthy because of his membership of the Communist Party of India. The ghost of Stalinism was still haunting the Soviet authorities. However, as the Soviet Union continued to open up, attitudinal rigidities were gradually discarded. When Habib left Tashkent, he was replaced by another Indian Sultan Hamid, who had earlier come to the Soviet Union when his uncle Khwaja Ahmad Abbas shot *Pardesi*, a film based on the life of Afanasi Nikitin, the Russian traveler to India in the fifteenth century. Sultan Hamid worked for two decades, till he died in 1981.

Additionally, to improve the quality of their Indian language experts, the Soviet Union, began sending them to India to hone their knowledge and proficiency in Indian languages especially Hindi and Urdu.

Simultaneously, the Soviet government invited Indian Professors to teach Hindi and Urdu to Soviet students so as to enable their students to grasp nuances of conversational and literary Hindi and Urdu.

Under this programme Prof Triloki Nath Dixit from Lucknow University came to Moscow to teach Hindi at the Moscow State University. Dr. Qamar Rais and Dr. B N Tewari arrived in Tashkent in September 1962 as teachers of Urdu and Hindi respectively. The latter two stayed in Tashkent for three years and laid firm foundations for Indian language studies in Tashkent.

The invitation to Professors of Hindi to teach the subject showed the realization that despite commonalities in grammar, vocabulary, speech, etc., the two languages had their independent identities. Hindi had a more wider reach than Urdu in terms of numbers, publications, administrative importance, etc. Hindi must be taught as an independent discipline. From now onwards, both languages were taught; students chose either of the two as their field of study though they read both. (Information supplied by Dr. Heike Liebau of Germany who studied Urdu during 1976-1981 in Tashkent)

Dr B.N.Tewari wrote a book on the language spoken by a migrant Indian community settled in Uzbekistan who had kept their mother tongue alive. A premature death prevented Dr Tewari from publishing more about his academic experiences in Tashkent.

Dr. Qamar Rais has maintained his contact with Tashkent as a teacher and in other capacities. He also developed interest in Uzbek literature and has translated several Uzbek literary works in Urdu.

With the passage of time the number of Indian languages taught in Tashkent was increased. Indian teachers, such as D. N. Sarkar, K.A. Faruqi, Q.O. Hashim, Surya Kumari, etc. taught here.[55]

The above-mentioned changes followed in the wake of recasting of Soviet foreign policy under Khurushchev, Secretary of the Communist Party of the Soviet Union, who was determined to open up his country especially to people from newly liberated countries. He hoped to enlist them as dependable allies in the ideological battle against capitalism. An important way to achieve this was to develop exchange of students between the Soviet Union and the newly liberated colonies. This led to an upsurge in oriental studies in the Soviet Union.

The ex-colonies were educationally backward, especially in fields of science and technology. Expectedly the ex-colonies grabbed the Soviet offer. The Indian response was enthusiastic.

The Soviet and the Indian governments agreed upon an exchange programme of students. The Soviet government offered scholarships to Indian students, proceeding to the Soviet Union. By late 1950s, Indian students started arriving in Moscow for postgraduate studies, mostly in science and technology. The first batch reached in 1959. It consisted of Madhusudan V. Oak, Prem Bhatnagar and Hazurbar. The first two were sent by the Home Ministry to develop their skill in Russian language. Huzurbar was a Mathematician. In exchange the Soviet government sent six students to India, three from Russia and three from Uzbekistan to Delhi, to hone their skills in Hindi and Urdu. Among Uzbek students was Fatih G. Teshbaev, who served Soviet establishments in India in various capacities between 1969-70 and 1979-84 and was independent Uzbekistan's envoy to USA. [56]

In course of time, many Soviet (including Central Asian) students studied Urdu at the Universities of Lucknow and Jamia Milia. Abidov, now Head of the Department of South Asian Studies at the Institute of Beruni, Tashkent, received his education at the University of Lucknow. (Information supplied by Ms.Dilaram, a research student from Tashkent at Bhatkhande Institute of Music, Lucknow). Some students, such as Faraghat Nadieva from Leninabad (in Tajikstan) studied language at

Jawaharlal Nehru University, New Delhi.

Several students from Central Asia in the post-Soviet era studied Hindi at Kendriya Hindi Sansthan, Agra. Among these mentioned may be made of Dilaram, Mabzuda Sadikova (from Uzbekistan) and Nigina Babajanova and Faraghat Nadieva (from Tajikistan). The latter as stated above had earlier studied Hindi at Jawaharlal Nehru University, New Delhi.

The Soviet programme of inviting students from newly liberated colonies was designed as a powerful tool for propagating Soviet ideology of anti-racism, anti-colonialism and anti-capitalism. This became evident when in 1960 the Soviets opened the Friendship University at Moscow (soon to be renamed as Patrice Lumumba Friendship University) with a view to enrolling students in undergraduate and postgraduate courses from the newly independent countries of Asia, Africa and Latin America, in science, technology and medicine. Absence of trained man-power in the sphere of science and technology prevented ex-colonies from embarking upon a course of modernization and economic development.

The Soviet gesture was welcomed and immediately lapped up by underdeveloped countries. Students started arriving in the Soviet Union from former colonies.[57] The University imparted graduate and postgraduate education to students from 45 African, Asian and Latin American countries in humanities, social sciences, science, technology , medicine, etc. between 1965 and 1990. The single largest beneficiary of this programme was India; during this period more than 700 Indian students completed their courses in different discipline successfully.[58]

The Soviet policy of inviting foreign students created one problem. The newcomers, ignorant of Russian language, the medium of instruction, needed to be taught the basics of Russian language before they entered any Soviet educational institutions. Tashkent was one place where such a center was located for students coming from the Middle East, South Asia and Southeast Asia. The Institution was Podgotovitleny Fakultet Dlya Innostranikh Grazhdan (Preparatory Faculty for Foreign Citizens) under the auspices of Tashkent State University. From 1962 onwards batches of Indian students first acquired knowledge of Russian language in its precincts before joining institutions in Uzbekistan or in any other part of the Soviet Union.(The author was among the first batch of Indian students, who studied Russian language at this Faculty before joining Institut Narodov Azii, A.N., SSSR, Moscow (now Institut Vostokovedeniya) as a Ph. D. student.)

With the opening of the doors of Preparatory Faculty presence of Indian students in Tashkent became a constant feature; this has been maintained for over four decades even after the emergence of Uzbekistan as an independent, sovereign nation.

Indians around Tashkent further contributed to the strengthening of the teaching of Indian languages. The result was that in 1960s Tashkent emerged as a major center for teaching Hindi and Urdu in the Soviet Union, next in importance to Moscow and Leningrad (now Petersburg). According to Shamatov, proficiency in Indian languages enabled Central Asian scholars to take up major subjects of Indian history for their researches. Shamatov says, "The period after 1966 is marked by an upsurge of interest in Indian studies".[59] Shamatov's assessment is correct.

The two major centers that emerged in Tashkent for the study of Indian history, society, culture, languages and literatures were Institut Vostokovedeniya and Abu Reihan Al-Beiruni Istitute of Oriental studies, Academy of Sciences, Republic of Uzbekistan, both located in Tashkent. The former has a special section dealing with histories and literatures of 'foreign oriental countries'. The latter has a department named "Relations between the people of Central Asia and South Asia". Indological studies are carried on under the aegis of this department.[60]

The growing closeness between the Soviet Union and India impacted Central Asian cultural scene as well. In 1967 Uzbekistan declared the Decade of Indian Culture. Next year India reciprocated and declared a Decade of Uzbek culture in India.[61] These events were additional incentives to the development of Indian studies in Central Asia and particularly in Uzbekistan.

One result was that the teaching of Indian languages was

vastly improved in the institutions of Tashkent. The reputation of the Faculty for teaching Indian languages was such that it attracted students not only from the neighbouring Soviet Republics, such as Ukraine, Kazakhstan, Kyrgzstan, Tajikstan, Georgia, Azerbaijan, etc., but also from several Communist countries, such as Bulgaria, Poland, German Democratic Republic, Cuba, Vietnam and Mongolia, etc. Students from these countries came to study Hindi and Urdu. Some students wanted to improve their proficiency in these Indian languages. It was under this scheme that Leibau, a scholar from German Democratic Republic arrived in Tashkent in 1976 for studying and improving her skill in Urdu. Among German scholars she is still continuing her researches on Indian history and society.

Since Indo-Soviet ties, political, economic and cultural, were acquiring new dimensions, Soviet students (including Central Asians) after completing studies in Indian languages at Tashkent found employment in Soviet diplomatic services or Soviet-sponsored projects in India. Dr. Surat Mirkasymov, after completing his studies in Indian languages in Tashkent, worked as Soviet Consul in Calcutta (Kolkata) in 1970s; J. A. Khozbaeva, worked as Interpreter in Bhilai Steel Project[62] etc. Some were absorbed as teachers and/ or researchers in educational institutions in Tashkent or in neighbouring republics.

Visit to India to update their skills in Indian languages was an additional motivation for Central Asians to study Indian languages. Proficiency in Indian languages could provide an opportunity to work or study in India.

By early sixties, Central Asian scholars were linguistically well-equipped to carry on researches in Indian society, history and Urdu and Hindi literatures and philology.

In 1962, the Soviet policy makers made a significant decision. Gafurov emphasised that the Soviets wanted to promote an intensive study of modern and contemporary societies of the oriental countries. This policy decision gelled with the policy of laying stress on the study of languages of different countries with which the Soviets were expanding their political, economic and military relations.[63]

From Philology to Literature

Young scholars, now proficient in Indian languages were well suited to critically study contemporary Indian literature, especially works in Urdu and Hindi. This was also necessitated by the Soviet policy decision in 1958 to start a movement to 'unite progressive authors in Afro-Asian and Latin American countries'. The Soviet government chose a Central Asian, an Uzbek man of letters and poet, Gafur Gulyam to head this organization.

In India the ground for such a movement already existed. In 1936 Progressive Writers Union was organized with the famous Hindi litterateur Premchand as President. Most of the members were either sympathetic to Communism and the Soviet Union or members of the Communist Party of India. Those associated with Progressive Writers Union had no hesitation in joining the Soviet-sponsored Conference of writers from Africa and Asia held at New Delhi in 1956. Two years later, in 1958, Indian authors participated in the Conference of Afro-Asian writers held at Tashkent.[64] The organization became a new channel for forging intellectual and cultural links between India and Central Asia.

This movement aiming to bring litterateurs on one platform from ex-colonies could not ignore writers in Indian languages, especially in Hindi and Urdu. Soviet scholars (including Central Asian scholars) devoted themselves to the study of Indian literature. This was to understand and appreciate the dynamics of Indian society. From now onwards there was a continuous interaction between Central Asian and Indian authors.

The VIII Conference of Afro-Asian writers was organized in 1973 Alma Ata (now Almaty) in Kazakhstan. After the Conference was over, a 'round table' of authors from Uzbekistan, India, Pakistan and Bangldesh was convened at Tashkent to discuss the following issues:

a) the concept of progressivism in modern literature and art
b) social progress and culture
c) mass media of communication, writer and literature for masses
d) enlightening role of literature in the formation of scientific

ideology and awakening the masses to the importance of knowledge.[65]

Indian Literature

Central Asian scholars, in the first place, opted for studying modern and contemporary Indian literature. Simultaneously a publishing house was set up in Tashkent to bring out Russian and Uzbek translations of literary works of orient, including India.[66]

The study of literatures of Oriental countries outside the Soviet Union was boosted when a new sector was created in 1963 in the Institute for studying literatures of people of orient outside the Soviet Union under S. G. Rizaev, an Iranist.[67] Rizaev published in 1971 a monograph on Indian style in Iranian poetry from the end of the XVI to XVII Centuries.[68]

The list of Indian authors selected for research is long and impressive. However, before starting their studies, the Central Asian scholars had to ensure that the selected author was 'progressive'. They normally selected authors for study, who were either communists or fellow-travellers or associated with front organizations of the Communist Party of India. As time progressed the criterion was relaxed; authors not satisfying the criterion of 'progressivism' were also studied. Dissertations were written and monographs published on Krishan Chander, Khwaja Ahmad Abbas, Yashpal, Upendranath 'Ashk', Amritlal Nagar, Subhadra Kumari Chauhan, Ali Sardar Jafri, Ilachandra Joshi, Vishnu Prabhakar, Amrita Pritam, etc. [69]

Indian society and culture have found reflection in the creative writings of Central Asian litteratuers such as Mirza Tursun-zade, Gafur Gulyam, Zulfi, Uigun, Aibek, Sharaf Rashidov, Erkin Vahidov, etc.[70]

As the study of individual authors progressed, some researchers shifted their focus: they would chalk out dominant literary trends, in different Indian languages. Polinova's work *Realism v sovremennom indiiskom romane* [71] reflects this emphasis. In this work she has examined the writings of Tagore, Prem Chand, Krishan Chander, and Yashpal,etc. Her monograph treats 'the problem of realistic approach in Hindi, Urdu and Bengali literatures.'[72]

Polinova's students, Drs R. Ghulyamova and N.A. Khojaeva have studied Vishnu Prabhakar and the Punjabi authoress, Amrita Pritam.[73]

Experience gained in literary studies emboldened some Central Asian scholars to take up topics in philology.

Dr. S. A. Chernikova's book on compound verb in Urdu was published in India. Dr. Khejaeva's critical study of Amrita Pritam came out in Punjabi language in India. [74]

Most of these studies were published in Russian language. Some authors sought the medium of Uzbek language to express themselves. As a result of these publications in Russian and Uzbek languages, Uzbeks became familiar with contemporary Indian literature and literary trends in modern India.

Another agency now emerged to deepen and expand cultural relations between the two countries.

The Soviet government encouraged the establishment of Indo-Soviet Cultural Societies or ISCUS; they set up its counterpart in its own country. (The lineage of ISCUS could be traced to the society named as Friends of the Soviet Union, established in India in 1941, to show Indian people's solidarity with Soviet citizens when their country was attacked by Hitler during the second world war.) These Societies regularly sponsored mutual visits by scholars, cultural activists and distinguished citizens.

Each of the Soviet Central Asian Republics individually established special relationship with one of the Indian states. For example, Uzbekistan and the Punjab and Kyrgyzstan and Bihar entered into special relationships with each other and became brother states.[75] Regular contacts with foreigners unleashed in Central Asia a strong desire to study their own history and culture intensively. As a part of this exercise, local historians began to study international contacts of their region in historical perspective. Earlier the existence of these contacts was known but now they emphasized these relations to affirm that their ancient civilization was not insular and the present exercise of reaching out was but a continuation of a hallowed tradition. These studies pointed to a continuous exchange of commodities, persons and ideas with their neighbours throughout history. Economic, cultural and religious ties with people beyond their borders were an integral part of their history. Now when they were again reaching out to the world at large, historical studies of past relationships seemed logical and relevant. The government supported these researches in order to buttress the theory of friendship and brotherhood of all mankind, they were propounding. However these studies were carried out with certain "inbuilt precautions'. Unpleasant facts had to be glossed over. Nevertheless, this perception led Central Asian scholars to study the history of people around their country, sometimes directly and sometimes indirectly. In case of India the studies were both direct and indirect.

Uzbekistan: Historical Studies

India and Central Asia have been in touch with each other since ancient times. Indians have been visiting lands beyond the Oxus, stretching from the Caspain Sea to the Pamir plateau and receiving visitors from these parts. In modern terms this region roughly consisted of the Central Asian Republics of Azerbaijan, Turkmenistan, Uzbekistan, Kyrgygzstan and Tajikistan. Lying along the silk route in ancient times, these countries had trade relations with India; Buddhism reached these lands from India in the first millennium of its existence.

History showed that Central Asians had off and on invaded India and once in a while, carved out an empire for themselves.

Search for the Timurid Heritage

In Uzbekistan, the search and reassertion of their Timurid heritage should be seen as an offshoot of this thinking. In the process the Central Asian scholars necessarily focused on sources pertaining to medieval Indian history, mostly in Persian languages, available in the manuscript libraries of their country.[76] History had ordained that among the Central Asian Republics, the most vivid memory of India should be preserved among the Uzbeks. One of their greatest conquerors and empire builder was Timur, who had invaded India in 1398; his capital Samarkand was built with Indian booty and craftsmen. The extant grand monuments of Samarkand were constant reminders to Uzbeks how one of their former rulers had vanquished India.

The studies on Timur began with a look on contemporary Persian chronicles. Some of them were translated into Russian and Uzbek languages so as to make them accessible to a wide range of researchers and readers.

These researches showed that Timur on his return from campaign in India in 1399 brought fabulous booty, a large body of craftsmen and slaves. These craftsmen were employed in the construction of architectural monuments. These buildings reminded the locals of their historical contacts with Indians and India. They also provided a firm starting point for a study of Indo-Uzbek relations in medieval times. It was clear that from now onwards Indo-Uzbek relations were a part of academic studies.

The Timurid ruler of Herat, Shah Rukh, sent Abd-Ar Razzaq, an envoy to the south Indian kingdom of Vijayanagar in 1441-42. On his return journey Abd-Ar Razzaq was accompanied by an embassy of the Indian ruler.

Indo-Uzbek ties were mutual, not unidimensional.

Once in Herat, Abd-Ar Razzaq penned "Matla 'al-Sadayn", a chronicle of contemporary events, a history of the Timurids and a detailed account of his voyage to India and back.

Asam Urunbaev defended his Candidate's dissertation on a portion of Razzak's work: Razzaq's journey to India (1442-44) and back. He published the relevant portion in original Persian and its translation in Uzbek from Tashkent in 1960.[77] He brought out a Uzbek translation of Razzaq's work in Tashkent in 1969.

Early in the XVI Century another scion of the Timurid House, Babur arrived in India to establish Mughal dynasty, one of the longest-lasting ones in Indian history. Babur, besides being a conqueror, was also a poet and a writer. His autobiography besides being a literary gem is also a fine all round description of both Central Asia and India. Its study throws light on the renewal and strengthening of contacts between India and Uzbekistan.

Uzbek scholars searching for Timurid heritage repeatedly consulted contemporary accounts and in the process unearthed valuable data throwing light on Indo-Central Asian links.

Zahiruddin Muhammad Babur established the Mughal Empire in India after defeating Ibrahim Lodi at the first battle of Panipat in 1526. The new conqueror, Babur did not follow in the footsteps of his predecessor Timur; he did not return to Central Asia or Afghanistan; he settled down in India; neither he nor his successors (except Shah Jahan, who unsuccessfully tried to incorporate Central Asia into his Indian Empire in the mid-seventeenth century) ever returned to Central Asia. However, none of the Mughal ruler forgot the home of ancestors; they remained in regular touch by a variety of means. They sent gifts to shrines, held in esteem by their ancestors; they dispatched and received diplomatic missions; they promoted trade between the two areas; they welcomed scholars from Central Asia in their courts; they recruited Central Asians as soldiers and officials in the state service at all levels etc. India remained fresh in Uzbek memory.

S. Azimdzhanova, Director (1950-1977), Institute of Oriental Studies, Academy of Sciences, Uzbek SSR, concentrated her researches on the life and career of Babur. It was her obsession; she produced several monographs and papers on the topic. It is said Azimdzhanova wrote on everything concerning Babur, except on his poetry and coinage.

She was the Editor-in-Chief of the first Russian translation of Babur's autobiography.[78] The work was a major step forward in search for independent Uzbek identity; it also showed that Indo-Uzbek relations from the sixteenth century onwards were continuous and multi-faceted despite political changes in both the areas.

Azimdzhanova's other writings on Babur were *Ferghana under Umar Sheikh Mirza and Babur* (in Russian)(her dissertation for Candidate's degree), *Gosudarstvo Babura v Kabule i v Indii,* 1984 (Babur's rule in Kabul and India), her Doctoral dissertation and Babur's Divan entitled *Indiiskii Divan Babura,*[79] etc.

Other Central Asian scholars supplemented Azimdzhanova's efforts. A. M. Mukhtarov of Tajikstan wrote on inscriptions containing Babur's name at Matche and about other inscriptions found in the upper reaches of Zarafshan.[80]

Uzbek scholars made the study of Timurid legacy on the basis of contemporary chronicles a major academic activity.

A logical corollary was the publication of the Uzbek translation of memoirs of the daughter of Babur, Gulbadan Begum's *Humayunnama* in 1959. Azimdzhanova and Baikova contributed a Foreword to it.[81]

Babur-Name and *Humayunnama* are also important as sources for a student of medieval Indian history; these works give an insight into Babur's career and achievements before he became the ruler of India. They also portray the socio-economic and political condition of India and Central Asia. The study of Central Asian and Indian scholars both supplemented and complemented each other. The most important conclusion was that portrayal of various aspects of Indo-Central Asian relations was feasible on the basis of contemporary data and should be promoted in the context growing friendly relations between the two countries.

The hypothesis was confirmed when Soviet scholar A. A. Semenov translated Munshi Muhammad Yusuf's medieval work in Tajik into Russian as *Mukim Khanskaya Istoriya.* Published in 1955, it revealed that a thriving colony of Hindu traders existed in Uzbekistan in the seventeenth century.[82] Central Asian scholars were indirectly encouraged by this revelation to develop the theme of the presence of Indians at length. Some Uzbek historians extensively worked on this topic in the sixties.

One more achievement of Central Asian scholars is their translation of Al Biruni's 11 Century Arabic work *Kitab fi tahqiq ma li'l-Hind* into Russian in 1963 as *Indiya.*

A.B.Khalidov and Yu. N. Zabadovskii translated the text. V.A. Arman and A.B.Khalidov provided notes and extensive commentaries. Famous Soviet Arabist V.I. Belyaev was the Editor-in-Chief.[83] Readers noted that one of the Central Asian scholars, almost a millennium ago had spent years in India; he learnt Sanskrit and extensively studied scientific, philosophical and religious texts. He had interacted with Indians. His observations were trustworthy and constituted a major primary source for study of India's society and intellectual achievements in early medieval India.

Contacts with India and Indians

A step forward in discovering Indian connections was N. V. Baikova's work *Rol Srednii Azii v Rusko-indiiskikh Torgovlykh Svyazakh (Pervay Polovina XVI— Vtoray Polovina XVIII V.),* published from Tahkent in 1964. The work delineates Indo-Central trade relations from the sixteenth to the eighteenth century on the basis of Russian language and local source materials. The choice of this theme was due to preoccupation of Soviet historians with economic factors. Perhaps, this is the first systematic account of trade between the two regions during this period. It supplemented our knowledge of India's commercial contacts beyond her borders by the land route. We know about India's maritime trade during this period with countries extending from the east coast of Africa to Southeast Asia in much grater detail. This work reminded us that India and her neighbours across the land-frontier were also carrying on trade, defying rigours of journeys across, mountains, deserts and rivers. An year earlier, she had written an essay on Caravan trade between north India and Central Asia in the nineteenth century.[84] Baikova pioneered the study of this long neglected aspect of Indian history.

By G.L. Dmitriyev (Dmtriev) carried out an important research during this period; he wrote a thesis in 1965 on Indians in Russian occupied Central Asia in the second half of the nineteenth century and the early years of the twentieth century. The thesis has not been so far published but in course of time articles, based on different chapters did emerge.

The author's merit is that he extensively consulted archives in Uzbekistan and other parts of the Soviet Union; he also read official and non-official Russian-language publications on the topic. It is the most authoritative account of the activities of immigrant Indians in Tsarist Central Russia.

His article "From the History of Indian Colony in Central Asia"[85] shows that between 6 and 8 thousand Indians lived in Central Asia during the late nineteenth century. He explodes the myth that these Indians were mainly from Shikarpur (now in Sindh—Pakistan). Indians came from Peshwar, Multan, Lahore, Amritsar, Ludhiana, Kashmir, Delhi, Allahabad, Bombay, etc.

They were to be found in most of the towns of Tsarist Central Asia and the Emirate of Bukhara. They were engaged in various professions, trade, moneylending, agriculture, etc. Generally they did not bring their families. They lived together and publicly celebrated some of their religious festivals. The bodies of deceased Hindus were cremated. His thesis, when published, would be a great contribution to the history of Indian migration to Central Asia in the nineteenth century.

The afterword in the story was added when the Russian translation of the memoirs of the Tajik poet and author Sadriddin Aini was published in 1974.[86] Sadriddin Aini, who lived in Bukhara in 1890s and had contact with Indian Hindu traders presents a vivid picture of their social life. They lived in four *Serais* and numbered a few hundred. In the afternoon, they would drink a preparation made from the leaves of a narcotic plant *Bhang*, brought from India. Some of them would get high and indulge in drunken brawls.

The Emir of Bukhara tolerated them as moneylenders because he considered them to be 'an integral part of economy'. They were permitted to travel all over the Emirate.

Once the Tsarist authorities converted Bukhara into a Protectorate, Hindu traders faced a number of disadvantages. Their movements were restricted; their taxes were enhanced.[87] P.N. Rasul-zade's monograph *Is Istorii Sredne-Aziatsko-Indiiskikh Svyazei Vtoroi Poloviny XIX- nachala XX Veka*, published from Tashkent in 1968 recounts the story of economic and political contacts of Tsarist Central Asia with India till the beginning of the twentieth century and also describes various Indian missions, arriving in Central Asia in search of Tsarist support against their alien British rulers. We also learn that some Uzbek intellectuals such as Furkat published articles on India in the Uzbek press. It is a story of politico-economic and cultural contacts.

In the following year, i.e. in 1969 Il'ias Nizamutdinov published his work *Iz istorii Sredneaziatsko-indiiskikh otnoshenii (IX-XVIII vv.)* (From the History of Central-Asian –Indian relations (IX-XVII Centuries) in Tashkent. He carried the story back to the early years of Abbasid Caliphate when Caliphs Harun

Rashid and Mamun invited Indian scholars to Baghdad and the Islamic world came to know of Indian achievements in the realm of science (astronomy, arithmetic, medicine, etc.) and literature. Central Asian scholars, including Farghana-born Alfaraganu and Samarkand-resident Ahmad bin Muhammad Sugani studied advances made by Indian scholarship in different branches.[88]

Succeeding Central Asian scholars continued the tradition; with the establishment of the Delhi Sultanate an uninterrupted flow of Central Asian scholars to India began. They contributed immensely to the growth of Persian literature. The process was carried forward under the Great Mughals. Nizamutdinov presents a long list of Central Asian intellectuals who found patronage in Mughal India.

Nizamutdinov for the first time used twenty diplomatic and official documents relating to Indo-Central Asian commerce and ambassadorial exchanges.[89]

By 1970, Baikova, Rasul-zade, Nizamutdinov and Dmitriev had successfully outlined the contours of Indo-Central Asian contacts over the past millennium. It was also clear that diplomatic relations were supplemented by people to people exchanges. There was a continuous flow of ideas and commodities in both the directions.

In the coming decades more data were collected to make the picture complete.

The search for heritage prompted Central Asian scholars to take a look at Afghanistan, sandwiched between India and Central Asia. Afghanistan was the corridor, the Indians and Central Asians used during their outward journeys. This research threw further light on relations between the two regions.

Historian Baba Khojayev's researches on Central Asian relations with adjoining Afghanistan shed new light on the activities of Indian traders in this country after Afghanistan ceased to be a part of India administratively and politically in the eighteenth century. In his work *Russko-Afghanskiye Torgoviye-Ekonomicheskiye Otnosheniya Vo Vtoroi Polovine XVIII – Nachale XXv.*, Tashkent, 1965, written on the basis of mainly Russian language and Central Asian sources (rarely used by Indian researchers), we learn in detail about the activities of Indian traders and their role as mediators in Indo-Central Asian trade

Baba Khojayev also studied the history of Afghanistan in the twentieth century. His essay, "Missiya Gidermaier-Gentiga v Afghanistane (1915-16)" in *Kratkiye Soobsheniya Instituta Vostokovedeniya, AN, SSR, Moskva,1960, pp.18-26*, portrays the activities of Indian freedom-fighters during the first world war who wanted to put an end to British rule in India. Raja Mahendra Pratap, an Indian revolutionary accompanied this mission, sent by the German ruler Kaiser and set up a Provisional Government of India in Kabul in December 1915.

Baba Khojayev has mostly used sources available in Russian and Central Asian archives and therefore is able to convey the Russian side of the story of the 'Great Game' indulged in by both the British and the Tsarist authorities in Central Asia throughout the nineteenth century.

Along with looking for links between India and Uzbekistan, a small band of local scholars, Hashimov, Kasymov and Kutina took up purely Indian history themes for their researches. This was important as it signified that Indian history by itself had emerged as an academic discipline in Central Asia.

Kasymov published a monograph entitled Borba *Maisura za Nezavimost v Kontse XVIII v.* (Mysore's fight for independence at the end of the XIX Century) in Tashkent. It was also his dissertation for Candidate's degree in history. Later on he drifted to a study of Turkish history.[90] Kutina was interested in political institutions developing in India in the post-1857 period eventually leading to the formation of Indian National Congress in 1885. Kutina, later co-authored with Hasimov a major work, *Deytelnost Indiiskogo Natsionalnogo Kongressa I Obshchestvennogo Organizatsii Indii Kontse XIX i Nachalo XX V.* (Activities of the Indian National Congress and Social Organisations in India at the end of XIX and beginning of XX Centuries). The book was published in Tashkent in 1988.

Kutina also studied growing relations between India and Uzbekistan and carried forward the tradition of Baikova and Rasulzade. Her brochure *Ekonomicheskiye Svyazi Uzbeksitana c Indiyei* (Economic Relations Between Uzbekistan and India), written with the cooperation of Rasulzade showed that under the Soviet regime from 1960s onwards economic relations took an upward turn and Indians also launched economic projects in Uzbekistan.

These publications acquainted Uzbek intelligentsia with the course of Indian history at a time when relations between India and the Soviet Union were drawing closer and closer. Since most of these works were published in Russian language, the local elite, having received its education through the medium of Russian language, got acquainted with its past. This was in general true of the medieval period, whose history is known through Arabic and Persian chronicles. By mid-sixties, a genuine effort was on to put oriental studies on a sound footing and in the process Indian studies also received a boost.

Impetus to Indian Studies

Two events around this time helped the growth of oriental studies and Indian studies in Central Asia. First, in January 1964 the XXVI World Congress of Orientalists was held in Delhi. A strong contingent of scholars from the Soviet Union led by Bobojon Gafurov and Zhukovsky attended it. The Soviet contingent had several scholars from Central Asian Republics, such as S.Azimdzhanova, Ilyas Hasimov, Abdulgani Muhammedovich Mirzoyev, Akhror Mukhtarovich Mukhtarov[91] etc. The trip enabled Tajik and other Central Asian scholars to interact with their Indian and international colleagues working on medieval Indian history and growth of Persian language and literature in India.

After the Congress was over, Ilyas Hasimov delivered lectures in India and Pakistan.

The Soviet government under various agreements with the Government of India and University Grants Commission and other research institutions in India started sending scholars for field trips. The Indian government and institutions under bilateral agreement were permitted to send their scholars to the Soviet Union and Central Asia for short visits. The increased interaction between Indian and Central Asian scholars gave a further fillip to Indian studies.

The other event influencing the course of Indian studies was related to the Indo-Pakistan summit held at Tashkent through the mediation of the Soviet Prime Minister Kosygin in January 1966 in the aftermath of Indo-Pakistan War of 1965. Prime Minister Lal Bahadur Shastri of India and President Ayub Khan of Pakistan reached an agreement to discuss matters of mutual concern and it seemed that the relations between the two countries would become normal. Unfortunately, the same night Prime Minister Lal Bahadur Shastri passed away after a massive heart attack. India plunged into grief.

The Tashkent Conference was etched on Indian consciousness. To show solidarity with the people of India in the hour of their grief and to honour the deceased Indian Prime Minister, the city of Tashkent named a school after him; they also introduced Hindi as a subject in schools in Tashkent. The death of the Prime Minister on the soil of Tashkent brought India and Central Asia emotionally and intellectually nearer to each other and a new stage in Indian studies in Central Asian Republics and the Soviet Union started. This phase roughly lasted till the opening years of 1970s.

Engagement with Indian studies in the neighbouring Republic of Tajikstan also prospered though the focus was different.

Tajikistan: Indian Persian Literature

As a Persian-speaking area, the Tajiks concentrated more on researches in the history of Persian language and literature. In medieval India, Persian was the language of administration and international trade and inter-state communication and diplomacy. As a result Persian received extensive court patronage; it became a language of elite discourse. Persian language and literature flourished in this country. Persian-speaking Iranis, Afghans and Tajiks were warmly welcomed in India. Scholars in Tajikistan hoped that by studying the growth of Persian literature in India they would better understand history of the development of Persian on the Indian subcontinent. In the process they also expected to map out the fortunes of their compatriots who migrated to India.

Hence, studies were carried out on Amir Khusro Dehlevi, Faizi, Bedil, etc. [92] All these Persian poets flourished in medieval India.

By now the Central Asians were sure that manuscripts of writings of their writers could be found in India if a proper search was made. The fruition of this dream took place when both the countries came further close during 1970s. A mission of Uzbek scholars from the Academy of Sciences visited India during March-April 1975 and discovered 242 manuscripts on 'history, literature and culture' of Central Asia. At the end, of 1976 another mission from Uzbek Academy of Sciences arrived in India. It visited depositories in cities such as Delhi, Calcutta, Haiderabad, Lucknow, Rampur, Patna, Alwar, Jaunpur and Mysore. It microfilmed several manuscripts of interest to Central Asian scholars. All these activities further promoted interest in intellectual links between India and Central Asia and motivated Central Asian scholars to take up Indian studies.

By mid-sixties, a genuine effort was on to put Oriental studies on a sound footing and in the process Indian studies also received a boost.

Several new dimensions to Indian studies were added. The most important component was the beginning of the study of Indo-Central Asian relations in the ancient period.

At the initiative of Bobojon Gafurov, an International Conference on Kushan studies was organnised in 1968 at Dushanbe, the capital of Tajikistan.[93] It should be remembered that the Kushanas in the first century A.D. emerging from Central Asia ruled over a territory forming a part of both their homeland and India. Their contribution to Indian culture, religion and art is an integral part of Indian civilization. Some of the scholars who participated from the Indian side were Prof R.S. Sharma, Prof. G.C.Pandey, Prof. Devendra Kaushik, etc.

The Kushanas had played an active role in propagating Buddhism in Central Asia. It was necessary to study the growth of Buddhism in Central Asia. The Indian religion flourished for several centuries and contributed extensively to the local culture. This was an additional cultural link between India and pre-Islamic Central Asia. It was necessary to study the growth of Buddhism in order to appreciate the nuances of pre-Islamic Central Asian culture. The topic had not received due attention till then at the hands of Soviet (including Central Asian) scholars. In the aftermath of the Conference, international attention was focused on the culture of pre-Islamic Central Asia and soon scholars took up Central Asian Civilisation as a part of their collective research.

The interest in the study of spread of Buddhism in Central Asia led to a realization that a study of the growth of Civilisations in Central Asia should be taken up jointly by the Soviet and other scholars of the world. Soon UNESCO became involved in the project. Study of Central Asian Civilisations became a global enterprise. Experts on Central Asian history, civilization and culture from all over the world helped the enterprise.

Initially a study of the ancient silk route running from China to the Mediterranean Sea was taken up. Finally, a joint history of Central Asian Civilisation in several volumes was mooted. Bobojon Gafurov had ensured through his deft diplomacy that Central Asia would not remain a forgotten chapter of history among international academics.[94]

Prof. A. M. Mukhtarov and Prof Asimov from Tajikistan were closely associated with the execution of this UNESCO-sponsored project. As Fredrico Mayor, Director-General of UNESCO observed, "For same 1,500 years this arid inland sea far removed from the earth's true Oceans – was crucial as the route along which the merchandise (notably) silk and ideas flowed between China, India Iran and Europe."[95] An *ad hoc* International Scientific Committee was formed in 1980 to plan and execute the work. The UNESCO decided to sponsor a new project for the study of the Silk Route and also the history of Civilisation of Central Asia. Prof Asimov of Tajikistan (he was earlier Education Minister of Tajikistan) was appointed as one of the Vice-Presidents of the organizing committee.

It may be noted that from now onwards Asimov, like his fellow Tajik Bobojon Gafurov played an important role in propagating and promoting the study of Central Asian Civilisation under the auspices of UNESCO. He frequently visited India (1969,1971,1977,1981,) and was closely associated with international conferences concerning Central Asia (Dushanbe-1968, Samarkand-1969, Ashkabad-1972, Alma-Ata-1985, etc.). He immensely contributed to the UNESCO-efforts for promoting Central Asian Studies.[96]

Buddhist Studies

While UNESCO was trying to organize the writing of a multi-volume history of Central Asian civilisations, Soviet (including Central Asian) scholars energetically took to the study of the spread and development of Buddhism and other features associated with this phenomenon in Central Asia mostly on the basis archaeological excavations of Buddhist sites on their territory.

Scholars tried to understand the interaction between Indian art forms and Central art forms during the period when Buddhism flourished in Central Asia. The study attracted Soviet scholars from non-Central Asian parts as well.

The Soviet government also realized that Kalmyks and Buryat Mongols, citizens of the Soviet Union, who still professed Buddhism, would appreciate the study of Buddhism. This would also send positive message to the countries professing Buddhism in Southeast Asia and win their appreciation.

The first Soviet expedition to a Buddhist site had been organized long back in 1926. It had explored Kara Tepe in the vicinity of Termez on the banks of the Oxus river.[97] Thereafter little attention was paid to Buddhist sites.

In the post-Dushanbe Conference period, the Soviet institutions organized regular archaeological expeditions to Buddhist sites; their efforts brought to light several new Buddhist structures, extending in an arc from the Merv Oasis in Turkmenistan through Uzbekistan and Tajikstan, Kyrgyzstan. to southern Kazakhistan.[98] Of these sites Ajina Tepe in Vaksh Valley in southern Tajikstan, excavated between 1961 and 1976, is probably the most renowned site. It has frescoes, sculptures, inscriptions, etc., giving a bird's eye view of the Buddhist culture, then prevailing in Central Asia. It has a '12-metre clay figure of Buddha in *nirvanana* pose.'[99] For Indian students the conclusion is interesting "...It can be definitely said that in respect of composition and lay out "local monasteries were built mainly in accordance with Indian tradition."[100]

Another interesting conclusion is furnished by Stavisky who contends that Islam was established firmly only towards the end of the IX Century in Central Asia because till then several Buddhist sites continued to flourish.[101]

The exploration of these Buddhist sites provided a new opportunity for collaboration between Soviet (including Central Asian) and Indian archaeologists. Their reports have added new information to the spread of Buddhism and its history in the area. It was realized that coming of Islam to this area in the 7th century A.D. did not mean disappearance of Buddhism. It spread up to southern Kazakhstan between VII and X Centuries. Buddhism survived until finally it was overwhelmed by the repeated attacks mounted by Islamic armies.

The archaeological finds also include Buddhist texts, coins, clay tablets with inscriptions, etc. They all provide new material for study for students of Buddhism. These data confirm close cultural and trade links between India and Central Asia. These findings acted as a new motivation for Central Asian scholars for the study of Indian history and culture, both contemporary and past.

From this time onwards, Soviet scholars (including Central Asians) frequently came to India and undertook tours of different parts of the country and thus Indian studies started taking deep roots in Central Asian institutions.

Prof Bobojon Gafurov's initiative had resulted in deepening interest in Indian studies in the Soviet Union, especially in Central Asia. It was deeply appreciated in India. The Aligarh Muslim University conferred on him the D.Litt. degree *(honoris causa)* in 1970.[102]

1970s

In 1960s Indian studies had taken roots in Central Asia. In 1970s they flourished and really took off. Central Asian scholars diversified their field of studies; they moved away from the history of Timurid heritage or history of contacts or study of medieval Persian literature. The reason was a new stage in Indo-Soviet political relations consequent upon the signing of a new treaty of friendship on 9 August 1971. Mrs Indira Gandhi, the Indian Prime-Minister visited Moscow in September 1971 to reassert new closeness between the two countries.[103] The XXIV Congress of the CPSU ratified the treaty saying that the Soviet Union had either set up or was in the process of setting up 70 major projects and was therefore keen to strengthen its relations with India.[104]

Towards the end of 1971 India came still closer to the Soviet Union as war with Pakistan seemed imminent. India's anxiety was not Pakistan but the military and diplomatic support it received from the USA. The Soviet Union firmly sided with India during the Indo-Pak War of 1971. It rebuffed USA when the latter threatened to send its fleet to the Bay of Bengal at the height of Indo-Pakistan hostilities. India emerged victorious and Pakistan was dismembered; Bangla Desh was born as an independent and sovereign nation.

India was grateful for this help in its hour of crisis; the Soviets were convinced of the genuineness of India's policy of non-alignment. It was not a lackey of Western Powers. The two countries came together on a variety of international issues and friendship between the two attained new heights.

Leonid Brezhnev, the General Secretary of CPSU paid an official visit to India to symbolize the growing intensity of economic, political and diplomatic relations between the two countries. By mid 1980s, more than eighty big industrial projects functioned in India with Soviet co-operation.

The diplomatic closeness and government to government co-operation between the two countries further heightend Soviet scholarly interest in India. Indian studies now flourished in the Soviet Union (including Central Asia) as never before. Soviet and Central Asian scholars regularly visited India to update their studies and to interact with Indian specialists working in various institutions and universities. In Central Asia more and more Universities and Institutes opened their gates to Indian students. Earlier Indian students were mostly admitted to Tashkent University.

Tajikistan

In this decade Indian studies acquired the status of an independent discipline in Tajikistan, thanks to the interest taken by Bobojon Gafurov, who from the outset was clear in his mind that oriental studies should also be promoted in Soviet Central Asian Republics as culturally and historically both belonged to the Orient. Tajikistan had a tradition of oriental studies.

Gafurov pointed out that in Tajikistan oriental studies had begun in 1920s as a result of the efforts of distinguished Russian Orientalists V. V. Bartold, A. A. Semeinov, M. A. Andreev, etc. Tajikistan had a trained cadre of local oriental scholars as well.[105] Preliminary steps had been taken when the Soviets in late 1950s decided to promote oriental studies.

The Soviet Republic of Tajikistan established a sector of Oriental Studies in 1958.[106] Experts in different branches in Oriental Studies from Moscow and Leningrad had come to assist their Tajik colleagues in cataloging manuscripts and documents in possession of the Institute. They also assisted in collecting and microfilming manuscripts and documents available with individuals living in the hilly Badakshan region.[107]

The Institute published in 1960 and 1965 in two volumes the works of Amir Khusro (Khusrav Dehlavi).[108] Tajik scholars had turned their attention to India because of their interest in the development of Persian language and literature.

From this Sector emerged the first Indologists of Tajikistan, Abdullajan Gaffarov and Sharafbonu Pulatova.[109] It also published works of Mirza Ghalib and Allama Iqbal. [110]

In view of these achievements of the Sector, the Coordination Bureau on Academic Activities of Academy of Sciences in 1969 recognised that the Institute had significantly contributed to researches in Persian literature of north India and other countries.[111]

In 1970 the sector of Indian studies was upgraded and recognized as the Institute of Oriental Studies, Academy of Sciences, Tajikistan.[112] Subsequently an independent sector for the Study of India and Pakistan was organized under its auspices.[113]

The Institute took up the study of history of the evolution of India and Pakistan and also the study of literary achievements in Hindi and Urdu and a study of literary exchanges with neighbouring countries including India.[114]

The focus on Indian connection in Uzbekistan and Tajikstan led to an important discovery. Soviet ethnologist I.M.Oranskii during his field trip to the Hissar valley in Tajikistan found a community living in small groups and speaking neither Tajik or Uzbek, the two locally-spoken languages. On closer scrutiny he found that their in-group language of interaction was akin to Punjabi or Rajasthani, two Indian languages. This excited his interest and he investigated further. He found they were paria and all of them were illiterate. They were unable to state when their forefathers had come to this place. What was intriguing was that they had managed to preserve their language. Oranskii found that as a rule they married among themselves. If a member of their group married outside, the bride was persuaded to learn their language and use it in the household.

The discovery of this group showed that between India and Central Asia people to people contact even at the lowest level existed in the past.

Oranskii's article "K etnografii indoyazichnoi gruppy parya (Gissarskaya Dolina)" was published in D.L.Oldderogge, op.cit., pp.219-233.[115]

Asimov's Contribution

Asimov, like Gafurov, also played a decisive role in promoting Indian studies in this republic and indirectly helped popularsing them in the neighbouring Republics. With A. Mirzoev, he also published a brochure on Indian Persian poet Amir Khusro Dehlevi from Dushanbe in 1973. Thereafter he started studying Tajikistan's culture in the pre-Islamic period. He then emphasized researches in Kushan period and championed piecing together the Buddhist past. Asimov's efforts were highly appreciated in India. He was awarded the Nehru Prize in 1980.

His stand was clear in his essay, "Tsentralnaya Aziya v Drevnosti: Problemy Istorii I Kultury".[116]

Asimov as Vice-President of the UNESCO- Committee on Central Asian History and Culture came to Delhi to participate in a Seminar on Central Asia in 1992.

The Civil War raging in Tajikistan, following the disintegration of the Soviet Union in 1991, claimed him as one of its victims. He was assassinated in 1994.

Nevertheless Asimov's efforts had ensured that Indian studies, especially the study of Buddhism had taken deep roots not only in Tajikistan but also in Turkmenia, Uzbeksitan, Kyrgyzia and Kazakhstan. The unraveling of the Buddhist past in shape of *Viharas*, caves, sculptures, frescoes, terracotas, coins, texts, etc., showed that India and Tajikistan were bound by ties of a shared culture since ancient times.

In Tajikistan the trend of Indian studies was different from Uzbekistan. The Tajiks in the first place, mostly concentrated on the growth of Persian-Tajik language and literature on the Indian subcontinent. After 1968 when Kushan-studies were promoted, they concentrated on the study of the history of Buddhism in Central Asia; this theme became an important concern of scholars.

Some Tajik scholars showed interest in medieval Indian history. This was natural as Persian-Tajik speaking people they had no problem in studying medieval Indian chronicles, mostly written in the Persian language. Secondly, many of these medieval chronicles were available to them either in print or in manuscript. Thirdly, the Mughal Court was Persianised and had employed a number of Tajiks. They could learn about the part their forefathers played in the Mughal polity.

M. Vakoyev published in 1975 from Dushanbe a book on life and works of Amir Khusro and A. Gaffarov wrote on Persian Poetry in India and Pakistan in the second half of the nineteenth and early twentieth century (Dushambbe, 1975).[117]

Following the initiative of Bobojon Gafurov, scholars in Tajikistan, in 1970s also worked in close contact with scholars of other countries such as India, Pakistan, Afghanistan, Iran, etc.[118] In 1976 Nuruddin Jahangir's *Tazkirat-ul-Shaora* was published from Pakistan. The text was prepared by Prof A. M. Mirzoev. Next year A. M. Mirzoeva's text of Mutrib Samarkandi's memoirs of Jahangir was published with an afterword by M. Rashidi.[119]

Gafurov also aroused interest of Pakistani scholars in Mahmud b. Amir Wali's *Bahr al-asrar fi manaqib al-akhyar*, a world history written at the behest of Nazar Muhammad Khan by publishing an article about it.[120] An appendix describing Mahmud's travels in India and Ceylon (1624-31) entitled *Safarnama* was published from Karachi in 1980. Riazul Islam, a distinguished Pakistani scholar, edited this work. Ansar Zahid Khan published a number of articles on the basis of this travelogue in the *Journal of the Pakistan Historical Society*.[121] Mahmud extensively reports on religious practices, festivals and rituals of the Hindus. He writes about some strange practices. For example, he informs us about 'liver-eaters' or *jigar-khwar* of Orissa and Bengal. Mahmud's account is a good supplement to European descriptions of local customs and traditions of Bengal and Orissa.

Prof. A. M. Mirzoev died in 1976. Next year Bobojon Gafurov also passed away. After their death oriental studies became neglected in Dushanbe. Oriental studies including Indian studies had lost two important guides with the demise of these senior scholars. Nevertheless, some young scholars have continued their researches in Indian history.

Muzaffar Olimov wrote his Candidate's dissertation on Sindh. The title was "Agrarnoi Stroi Sinda, XVII-pervoi polovini XVIIIv.". In 1993 this was published as *Ocherki Istorii Sinda V XVII-Nachale XIX V.* (Essay on the History Of Sindh XVII-beginning of XIX Century).

The work is based on an extensive reading of medieval Indian chronicles on Sindh, supplemented by a study of European travelogues of the period. It presents a compact picture of agrarian economy, crafts, urbanization and commerce of Sindh during these centuries.

In Tajikistan, as had happened in Uzbekistan almost three decades back, the interest in Indian connection eventually fructified in the publication of B.I. Iskandarov's work *Srednayaya Aziya I Indiya* in 1993 from Dushanbe. The book mainly focuses on Tajikstan's relations with India and is based on printed and manuscript sources available on the territory of the former Soviet Union. It seems India had close business contacts with Tajikistan. A large number of Kashmiri merchants visited Tajikistan. Geographical proximity and availability of a number of routes enabled Kashmiri merchants to cross into Tajikstan. Indian currency circulated in Tajikstan till the beginning of the First World War. To date this remains the most authentic account of Indo-Tajik relations.

Uzbekistan: The Study of Indian Thought

Indian studies in Uzbekistan during 1970s acquired new dimension. An Indian scholar, Dr. Devendra Kaushik, based in Tashkent, published *Central Asia In Modern Times A History From The Early Nineteenth Century*, the first by an Indian. The data were collected from primary documentary sources in Russian language, available in Soviet archives. It was published in the Soviet Union in 1970. In Chapter V, the author discussed the relationship between Tsarist Central Asia and India and showed that Indians had been regularly visiting Central Asia to seek Russian aid in their struggle against their colonial British masters. In order to stop Indians from enlisting Russian support, the English rulers raised the 'bogey' of Russian invasion on India. The author had proposed a new reason for Russo-phobia, promoted in India in the nineteenth century by the ruling Englishmen.

The pro-Indian Soviet policies in 1970s and growing contacts between India and Central Asia were reflected in newer publications on India. They touched new areas of Indian society.

Central Asian scholars had made a shift in their study of Indian history in the beginning of 1970s. This is reflected in an anthology published from Tashkent in 1971, entitled *Ocherki istorii peredvoi obshchestvenno-filosofiskoi mysli narodov Zarubezhnogo Vostoka* (Essays on the history of advanced socio-philosophical thought of the people of foreign East).

In the section devoted to India, the authors discussed Raja Rammohun Roy, Mirza Ghalib, Sir Saiyyid Ahmad Khan, Swami Vivekanand, Bal Gangadhar Tilak, Mahatma Gandhi, Abul Kalam Azad and Jawaharlal Nehru, etc. The choice of thinkers is interesting; the Marxist Central Asian scholars no longer treated 'religious thinkers' or 'bourgeois thinkers' or those 'supporters of colonial master' as untouchables. They had realized that it was necessary to understand the role of those social activists who had influenced public opinion and shaped the course of events in Indian society in order to appreciate its dynamics.

Probably the success in maintaining democratic traditions and conducting a series of general elections and surviving three wars with Pakistan and a major conflict with China compelled the Soviet scholars to look for the ideology that had sustained India through these trying times. Other publications which followed confirm this trend. Another anthology exclusively devoted to political and ideological thought on the Indian subcontinent was published in Tashkent in 1976.

Entitled *Iz istorii progressivnom obshchestvennoi i filosofiskoi mysli v Indii* (From the history of social and philosophical thought of India), the book analysed prominent Indian thinkers, flourishing towards the end of the nineteenth and in the early twentieth centuries. Scholars underlined their role in bringing about modernization and the anti-colonial struggle.[122]

Thinkers discussed in this work included Sir Sayyid Ahmad, Swami Vivekanand, Muhammad Iqbal, etc. Special attention was paid to the growth of Marxist-Leninist ideas in India, especially in the post-November 1917 Revolution era. In this context the experience of the World Socialist Order was also considered. The conflict between the bourgeois and the socialist ideologies was explicitly described as a conflict between reactionary and progressive ideologies. The authors narrated the growth of Communist movement in India. They were keen to inform their readers that the Indian government was sympathetic towards the socialist world. This was probably the rationale for studying communist environment in India in detail.

It should be noted that the Central Asian scholars were paying attention to Muslim thinkers who had played a major role in shaping Muslim mind on the Indian subcontinent in the nineteenth and the twentieth centuries. Earlier they were ignored.

The growth of socialist thought in India was now at the

centre of attention of Central Asian academics.

M.B.Baratov published in 1973 *Leninism and Social Thought in India* in Uzbek language so as to acquaint his readers with the place and influence of Leninist ideas in the first half of the twentieth century in India amidst a maze of right, left, liberal, religious and fundamentalist ideologies. He sought to portray the impact of the Bolshevik Revolution on Indian national liberation struggle. He did not forget to point out the role of Taṣhkent in the growth of socialist ideas in India. After all, the first Communist Party of India was organized in Tashkent. The Association of Indian Revolutionaries formed in Tashkent unsuccessfully attempted to organise an armed attack on British India.[123]

The author was apt in summing up Nehruvian ideology: Nehru continued bourgeois politics but retained faith in socialism. His assessment was in keeping with the Soviet view of Nehru and the Soviet justification for the support given to Nehru.

The most significant departure made by Baratov was in the evaluation of Mahatma Gandhi. He pointed out that Gandhi had supported November Revolution and was 'a Great Humanist'.

Baratov published a number of articles in Uzbek language on Indian thinkers of the twentieth century, such as Vivekanand, Aurbindo Ghose, Rabindranath Tagore, Mahatma Gandhi, Radhakrishnan, etc.

Baratov's unforgettable contribution is, he brought the ideas of modern Indian thinkers to the Uzbek-language readers and made them aware of the richness and variety of modern Indian socio-religious thought.

The growth of Islamic ideology in the twentieth century-India now engaged the serious attention of Uzbek scholars.

Fatih Teshbaev, who wrote his Candidate's dissertation on philosophical and socio-political ideas of Sir Saiyyid Ahmad Khan published several articles. He also contributed an article on Maulana Abul Kalam Azad.

S.A. Yuldasheva wrote on the world-view of poet and thinker Dr. Muhammad Iqbal, often called the Father of Modern Pakistan.[124] The birth-centenary of Dr. Iqbal was celebrated at the Institute of Oriental Studies, AN, UzSSR.

The Uzbek readers were given a chance to understand the ideologues of Islamism on the Indian subcontinent as well. A major achievement of Central Asian scholars was that in 1970s works on Indian thinkers of all hues were available in Russian and Uzbek languages to Central Asian readers.

1980s: Indo-Uzbek Relations

Two important factors influenced the course of Indian studies in 1980s.The first was the rejuvenation of the organization of Oriental scholars, i.e. of All Union Congress of Orientalists of the Soviet Union, lying dormant since its first Congress in 1957.Credit for this belongs to Primakov, who later on became the Foreign Minister and subsequently the Prime Minister of independent sovereign Russia. He renamed it as Vse Souznaya Assosiatsiya Vostkovedov.The first congress of the new body was held in Baku in I983 in Azerbaijan. The next Congress was held at Dushanbe, the capital of Tajikistan in 1988.

The emergence of the new Association imparted a new sense of commitment to scholars in the field. It certainly spurred the Central Asian scholars to take up new areas for their researches, as will be seen presently.[125]

The second event was directly connected with India. In 1980s the Indian State acted as a sponsor of culture. It organized regional cultural centers and promoted traditional crafts. At the international level it sponsored Festivals of India jointly with the host countries.[126] Since India and the Soviet Union were politically very close to each other, a Festival of India was organized in the Soviet Union.

In the eighties the Uzbek scholars further enriched the corpus of Indian studies. The multi-dimensional nature of Indian studies in Uzbekistan becomes clear when we look through the pages of *Iz Istorii Kulturnykh Svyazei Narodov Srednei Azii I Indii* (From the History of Cultural Relations between Peoples of Central Asia and India), published in 1986 in Tashkent.

The book contains 19 articles covering a period beginning from ancient times through the medieval era to the contemporary period. The themes of essays are varied. The last paper traces the history of visits by Indian technocrats and academics since the sixties when academic cooperation between the two areas began to develop.

There are several papers illuminating different aspects of Indian history. B.A. Akhmedova's article "Mutribi I Ego Antologia (Mutribi and his anthology)" should have special appeal to students of Medieval Indian history.

Mutribi (See also Supra), a Central Asian scholar and poet visited the Court of Jahangir in 1625 at the ripe old age of seventy, accompanied by his son, Muhammad Ali. Jahangir saw his anthology, "Tazkirat-I-Shaura", an account of 320 Central Asian poets. The Emperor was greatly impressed by his scholarship. Jahangir presented him with the works of some more poets and wished that they shuld also be incorporated by him. Mutribi gave this collection a new name "Nuskha-I- Ziba-i-Jahangir". The names and works of these poets were preserved for the posterity.

Mutribi also wrote another work, "Khatirat-i-Mutribi (Recollections of Mutribi)", an interesting source for the study of Jahangir's reign. Abdulgani Mirzoev, a Tajik scholar in collaboration with Pakistani historians, Mahmud Hasan Siddiqui and Saiyid Hisamuddin Rashidi published a new edition of *Khatirat...* from Karachi in 1976-77. Both the works are 'important sources for the study of literary contacts between Central Asia and Northern India.'[127]

In eighties an important work came out. Of course, the writing was not devoted to India; it was an exercise to discover the medieval heritage of Uzbekistan but incidentally it shed important light on the activities of Indians in the sixteenth century in Samarkand. So far historians were not aware of this information from any other source.

The reference is to R.G.Mukminova's book *Sotsialnaya Differentsatsiya Naseleniya Gorodov Uzbeksitana v XV-XVI vv.* (Social differentiation among urban population in the cities of Uzbekistana in the XV-XVI Centuries, Tashkent, 1985). The book analyses data collected from unpublished *wakf* documents. We discover there were Indian weavers working in Samarkand on behalf of an Indian merchant, hailing from Lahore. The Indian merchant received the cloth woven by these weavers. He was very affluent and would lend money on interest to these weavers. This is the first contemporary detailed account of Indian craftsmen working in a foreign country. Mukminova has through her researches unveiled a hitherto unknown dimension of Indo- Uzbek relations.

The dawn of 1980s was also the height of Indo-Soviet friendship. In November 1986, Gorbachev was in Delhi. He and Indian Prime Minister Rajiv Gandhi issued Delhi Declaration proclaiming their identity of views on international affairs and signified that the two countries were coming further closer.

The government of Rajiv Gandhi organized Festival of India in Moscow in 1987. Prime Mnister Rajiv Gandhi and CPSU General Secretary Gorbachev attended the grand opening ceremony. The third phase of the Indian Festival was held in Tashkent. The commencement of the Festival was preceded by the opening of Indian Consulate in Tashkent with Yogendra Kumar as the First Consul of India. It was first Indian Consulate in the Soviet Union outside Moscow. The step showed the importance of Tashkent in the eyes of the Indian government in Central Asian region. Tashkent remains even today an Indian window on Central Asia.

The Indian government organized an Exhibition where Indian consumer goods were sold. Above all, the people of Tashkent were given an opportunity to see live performances by great maestros of Indian classical music and dance. Folk-artists from different parts of India also entertained the spectators. The show drew large crowds.

Indian publications were also sold in this exhibition. For the Central Asian scholars and public interested in India, this was the first opportunity to purchase Indian books on their soil. In Tsarist Russia Indian publications were sold in shops in Bukhara.[128] An Indian shop Ganga was opened where Indian goods were for sale. It was very popular. It closed down after Uzbekistan became a sovereign independent nation and import of Indian commodities became easier.

A work completed in 1980s in Tashkent but posthumously

published in 2002 in India in English translation, G.L.Dmtriev's *Indian Revolutionaries In Central Asia* is significant for the history of the Indian Revolutionary Movement in the colonial period from several angles.

Dmtriev, while preparing his study on Indian community in Tsarist Central Asia, read a large body of material in Russian and Uzbek languages and found that after the November 1917 Bolshevik Revolution, the role of Indian community in Central Asia had changed.

Two major factors were responsible for this. First, the Bolshevik economic policies did not leave any space for private trading. Secondly, in India Non-Co-operation and Khilafat Movements had created a lot of resentment against the British rule. The Muslims were especially dissatisfied with the treatment meted by the Allies to their Caliph. They started the Khilafat Movement. As per its programme, Muslims were asked to leave India in order to organize 'a war' against the British government. A substantial body of Muslims left India and reached Afghanistan where the Afghan King Amanullah promised them all support. On arrival in Afghanistan, the King under British pressure reneged on his promises. Some of the Indians decided to move to Tashkent where the Soviet rule, an implacable enemy of colonialism and imperialism, welcomed them with open arms. During the same period the Comintern after its Congress ended, had sent Indian revolutionaries M.N.Roy and Abani Mukerjee to create a base for Indian patriots for mounting an armed attack on India. Tashkent had thus emerged a major centre for Indian Revolutionary activities.

Dmtriev, on the basis of archival documents in Russian and Uzbek languages and contemporary Central Asian press, traces step by step, the activities of Indians from 1917 to 1921 in Tashkent till the Soviet government ordered Indian patriots to move to Moscow and withdrew all the facilities given to them.

The Soviets had opened a Military School to impart military training to Indians in 1920. A programme of lectures on political problems was initiated to educate the immigrant Indians. Things came to naught as Indian leaders failed to unite and often quarreled amongst themselves on trivial matters. The Soviets closed the School in 1921 and Tashkent lost its importance as a base for revolutionaries by the Indians.

Before he could prepare the final Draft of the manuscript, Dmtriev unfortunately passed away in 1987. The manuscript remained with his wife. Prof. Devendra Kaushik during one of his trips to Tahskent contacted Mrs Dmtriev and persuaded her to handover the manuscript. On return to India, he got it translated into English and published it on behalf of Maulana Abul Kalam Azad Institute of Asian Studies,(Government of India), Kolkata.[129]

A. A. Yuldashev, who had studied Urdu at the graduate level in 1986 defended a thesis on the question of social development and humanism in Jawaharlal Nehru's world view in Tashkent. In 1989 he published a brief biography of Nehru in Uzbek language. The author has clearly brought out elements of rationalism and humanism in Nehru's world view.[130]

In 1980s Uzbek scholars had started focusing on the study of modern Indian society, its ideological roots and the contours of its economy. Another dimension to Indian studies in Soviet Central Asia had emerged.

Abidov's work on Lala Lajpat Rai is a clear demonstration of this line of research. In the opinion of the author Lajpat Rai represented the anti-colonial feelings of the Indian society and also its national-democratic tendencies.[131]

Uzbek authors have also touched upon liberation movement among Indian women, the 'green revolution', economic exchanges between Uzbekistan and India, visits by scholars and distinguished citizens, etc.[132] In the process some burning issues confronting contemporary India have been touched upon.

In Tajikistan, Aziz Shvkatovich Niyazi wrote a thesis on the role of the *Mullahs* (Muslim Divines) in the social and political life of India, Pakistan and Bangla Desh.[133] As the title of the thesis suggests, the Central Asian scholars were now venturing into fields so long considered 'untouchable' in Indian studies in Soviet Indian historiography.

Other Central Asian Republics

Uzbekistan and Tajikistan, as we have seen, for historical reasons, actively promoted Indian studies. Scholars in other Central Asian Republics, such as Turkmenistan, Kyrgystan and Kazakstan having much less contacts with India in the past also tried to trace their historical links with India.

A scholar from Kazakstan, Beishembiev, prepared a critical study of 19th-Century Persian chronicle, *Tarikh-i-Shahrukhi*, written in 1870s in the Khanate of Kokand. The chronicle contains important information about Indians residing in Kokand during this period.

Some Indian soldiers had deserted the British army in the aftermath of the events of 1857 in India, had migrated to Central Asia and had joined the local armed forces. An Indian rose to the rank of commander of Kokand artillery. Abdul Majid, the British Agent in Kokand in 1860-61, calls him a Lahori, i.e. a resident of the Punjab.

The population of Andijan also had Chitralis and Peshawaris as its component.[134]

Beisembiev published another interesting article, "Ferghana's Contacts With India in the 18th and 19th Centuries" in *Journal Of Asian History* 28/2 1994, pp.124-35.

Articles on India were occasionally published in the local press in these republics since Indian presence was for one reason or other was always registered. As economic and political ties were strengthened there was a regular exchange of visits by Indians and citizens of these republics. Occasionally an Indian student studying in Lumumba University, Moscow would decide to spend his holidays in Kazakhstan as a member of Soviet Youth Team for participating in the programme "For the Development of Virgin Lands". We have the example of Arcot Moganavelu Punithavelu who came here in the summer of 1972. He was back again the following summer, but this time as a leader of the team. He won a Soviet Government medal for this.[135]

Many Central Asians worked in Soviet-sponsored projects in India. Before they made the trip, an orientation programme was organized for them. In this they were taught English and/or local

Indian language. A small group interested in India emerged, though they might not have been engaged in Indian studies.

On the education front, the Soviet government offered scholarships to Indian students to pursue higher studies in Soviet institutions.

In the seventies and eighties the number of Soviet scholars (including those from Central Asian Republics) coming to India increased.

Central Asian scholars mainly confined themselves to a study of the history of their own country in medieval and modern times; but they realized that the two countries were so closely bound that only by studying material available in Indian libraries and archives one could have a fuller understanding of Central Asian history in medieval and modern times.

It was time to move from a study of diplomatic and economic relations to realms of cultural exchanges as embodied in visits by scholars, litterateurs and artists, etc.

The increased interest in Indian studies was also sustained by a regular exchange of scholars and specialists between India and Central Asia. Some of the Central Asian scholars who visited India were Hasimov and Beisembiev, etc. Indian scholars who went to Tashkent were Devendra Kaushik, Mansura Haider, etc.

It is interesting to find that among Indian visitors to the Institute of Oriental Studies in Tashkent was a Professor Economics from Chandigarh, the present Prime Minister of India, Dr. Manmohan Singh. [136]

Other Aspects

As has been mentioned earlier, manuscripts of Indian literary works have been discovered in Central Asian libraries.[137] This shows that Central Asians were quite aware of the achievements of Indian writers in Persian language from the thirteenth century to the nineteenth century. The same may be said about Indians on the basis of the discovery of a number of text- books on Turkish grammar and multi-lingual dictionaries of Turkish languages. These dictionaries are from Turkish into Persian, from Arabic and Persian into Turkish, from Turkish into Urdu, etc.[138]

The author of one of the books on Turkish grammar book "Haft Akhtar" Kashi Lal appears to be a Hindu. He compiled the work in 1182 AH at the instance of his son in Persian language.

Ms. Dilaram informs me that there are dictionaries simultaneously containing Turkish, Persian, Pashto, Kashmiri, Punjabi and Urdu words. These were possibly prepared to help traders of both countries who frequented both India and Central Asia for purposes of trade.[139]

People to people contacts also generated a body of literature about which we so far know very little.

Conclusion

Indology in Central Asian Republics during 1950s to 1991 (the end of the Soviet Union) developed under the overall shadow of Soviet Indology. It confirmed to the direction and dictates of the Soviet ruling institutions.

Central Asian scholars in Indian studies received support from Indologists working in major centers such as Moscow and Leningrad. They went to these institutions, interacted with specialists and had access to their libraries and other infrastructural facilities.

Several Russian indologists and orientalists also contributed to the growth of Indian studies in Soviet Central Asia. Mention may be mode of Moskalev, I. D. Serebryakov, N. V. Baikova, etc.

Soviet governmental policies imparted the initial impulse. The Soviets in 1920s developed Tashkent as a listening post on Indian affairs and stationed their experts on India in Tashkent. As time progressed other factors, such as growing intensity of relationship between the two areas attracted more local students interested in learning Indian languages, especially Hindi and Urdu. Some of these later on took up Indian subjects for their researches. Their writings satisfied a large number of local readers, who had become interested in India that had thrown off an alien power and was rapidly modernizing itself and carving out a niche in world politics.

For historical reasons Uzbekistan and Tajikistan provided better opportunities for the development of indology than the neighbouring Republics of Turkmenistan, Kyrgyzstan and Kazakhstan. In this contribution of Bobojon Gafurov, the Director of Institute of Oriental Studies, AN, SSSR, for two decades was immense.

In Tashkent India studies revolved round four themes: Indo-Uzbek contacts, Indian history, Indian philosophical and social thought and Indian literature. In the initial phases, while studying Indo-Uzbek connection the emphasis was on economic interaction; gradually there was a shift to the exploration of educational and cultural contacts. Uzbek scholars primarily concentrated on a study of Urdu and Hindi litterateurs and philology. Among Hindi and Urdu authors they picked up those who were described by them as 'progressive'. With the passage of time 'non-progressive authors' were also studied. Some scholars also researched on the socio-philosophical thought as it developed on the subcontinent.

In Tajikistan, earlier studies were mainly concerned with the growth of Persian literature in medieval India since these also traced the growth of Persian-Tajik literature, the mother-tongue of the local population.

When archaeological excavations revealed Buddhist sites spread from Merv oasis across Uzbekistan, Tajikistan, Kyrghystan to Kazakhstan, Tajik scholars began studying Buddhist phase of Central Asian history and thus highlighted Indo-Central Asian interaction in spheres religion, culture, art, iconography, architecture, etc.

Sponsorship by UNESCO of a project to prepare a comprehensive history of Central Asian civilization across the centuries by international experts provided a new and powerful stimulus to Central Asian researchers to find their older contacts with their neighbours, including India.

The Uzbek and Tajik scholars thus helped to bring to light several facts relevant to the study of Indian history. They had popularized Indian studies in their republics.

By the end of 1980s, study of Indian society and history had emerged as an independent discipline. A bunch of qualified scholars were ready to promote, propagate and enrich it.

The disintegration of the Soviet Union in 1991 did not mean

a collapse of Indian studies in the former republics of the Soviet Union. The available bunch of experts has continued the tradition of Indian studies, but they are working within new parameters following the changed national and international political scenario. New strategic, political, economic, educational and cultural considerations have brought India and the newly independent, sovereign Central Asian Republics nearer to each other.

There was an awareness on both the sides to strengthen the existing relatonship to serve mutual interests. During 1992-93,Presidents of Uzbeksitan, Kazakhstan, Kyrghyzia and Turkmenistan visited India.[140] Indian prime Minister Narasimha Rao paid a return visit and announced the decision to establish Indian cultural centers in Tashkent and Bishkek and also substantial grants under Indian Technical and Economic Cooperation Programme. Thus a new beginning was made.[141] Indian Studies are being carried out in Central Asian republics with a renewed vigour.

India has opened Cultural Centres in Tashkent (Uzbekistan) and Bishkek (Kyrgyzstan) and Indian government has deputed eminent Professors to teach at Universities in both these cities. Professors Amin, B. Dey and S. Chakravarty have served in Tashkent.

The Indian government has sponsored scholarships for enabling Central Asian students to study or gain practical experience in Indian institutions and universities. Several students have made use of Government of India's offer and have studied (or are studying) in India.

It might be said that Indian studies are flourishing in Uzbekistan on a scale, not known in any other small country outside India.

Footnotes

1. P.M.Shastitko (chief editor), *Russko- Indiiskiye Otnosheniya v XIX v.(hereafter cited as R.-I. O v XIX V.)* , Moskva, 1997, doc. No. 137,p.303
2. A.I. Vygornitskii, *Posobiye dlya izucheniya yazika industani (Urdu) i voyenny* slovar *russko-industani,* Tashkent, 1898

3. M. Grulev, " Anglo-Russkiye otnosheniya na severo-zapadnoy grantise Indii", *Svedeniy kasayushiyesya stran sopredelnikh s Turkestan. Voyein.Okrugom* (hereafter cited as *Svedeniya)* , Tashkent 1898, vyp.4, pp. 14-21.
4. *Ibid.,* "Chitralskii Vopros", *Svedeniya,* Tashkent, 1898, Vyp.3, pp. 20-35.
5. *Ibid.,* " Belujistan I svyazanniye s nim voprosy", *Svedeniya,* Tashkent, 1899, Vyp,12. pp, 28-30.
6. G.G.Kotovskii (ed), *Bibliografia Indii, Moskva,* 1965 (hereafter cited as *Bibliografia...,*), p. 66, Nos. 1090, 1092 and 1094.
7. T.N.Zagorodnikov and P.M.Shastitko (editor-in-Chiefs) *Russko-Indiiskiye Otnosheniya v 1900—1917 gg.* (hereafter cited as *R-I.O. 1900-1917*) , Moskva,1999, p.122 f.n.17.
8. ICANAS—2004, *Brochure,* Moscow, 2004
9. I.P., Yagello, *Prakticheskay grammatika yazyika industani (urdu),* Tashkent, 1902; Ibid., *Industanii-Russkii Slovar, St. Petrsberg, 1902.*
10. *R-I.O. 1900-1917*, pp.114-22.
11. M. Grulev, " Pogranichniye zhelezniye dorogi v. Indii", *Svedeniya,* Tashkent, 1898, Vyp. 7, pp. 14-16.
12. *Ibid.,* " Zheleznodorozhnaya set v Indii i vopros o soedinonii yee s proyektiruyemymi zheleznymi dorogami v kitaye", *Svedeniya,* Tashkent, 1899, vyp. 11, pp. 8-12.
13. A.E. Snesaryev, " Zheleznaya doroga v Kashmir", *Svedeniya,* Tashkent, 1990, vvp.20, pp. 33-41
14. I. Yagello, "Torgoviye shnosheniya Indii s Persiyei", *Svedeniya,* Tashkent, 1904, vyp-53, No. 5, pp. 9-10; *Ibid.,* "Anglo-indiiskaya missiya v yugovostochnyu Persiyu", *Svedeniya,* Tashkent, 1906, Vyp.78, No5, pp. 12-17.
15. M. Grulev, "Anglo-Ruskiye otnosheniya na severo-zapadnoy grantise Indii", *Svedeniya,* Tashkent 1898, vyp.4, pp. 14-21.
16. *Ibid.,* "Chitralskii vopros", *Svedeniya,* Tashkent, 1898, Vyp.3, pp. 20-35.
17. *Ibid.,* "Belujistan I svyazanniye s nim voprosy", *Svedeniya,* Tashkent, 1899, Vyp,12. pp, 28-30.
18. *Bibliografia...,* p. 66, Nos. 1090, 1092 and 1094.
19. Losyev, "Togovlya c Zapadnym Tibetim (Industansko-tibetskii put)" *Svedeniya* Tashkent, 1906, vyp. 81, No. 8, pp. 16-31. Losyev also visited India in 1905 and submitted a Secret Report to the Tsarist Government. It was printed in 1908 at St. Petersberg, the capital of Russia. During his travels, he met the famous Indian

revolutionary Ajit Singh in Lahore. See Surendra Gopal, "The Travelogue Of A Russian Officer In India" in *Proceedings*, Indian Historical Records Commission, Vol. XLIII, Lucknow Session, 1975, pp.127-132.

20. *Bibliografia...,* pp. 180-181, Nos. 3119-3128.
21. *Ibid.,* p. 181, No. 3134.
22. Losyev, "Miting magometan v Bombye", *Svedeniya,* 1906, Vyp. 1, No. 8, pp. 32-33; Yagello, " Musulmane v Indii", *Svedeniya,* 1906, Vyp.83, No.10 pp. 17-23; *Ibid.,* " Indiskiye Musulmane i evropeiskaya kultura", *Svedeniya,* Vyp.79, No.3, pp. 24-25.
23. *Bibliografia...,* p. 181, No. 3133.
24. *Ibid.,* p. 148, No. 2540 and p. 161, No 2751.
25. C.D.Miliband, *Bibliograficheskii Slovar Otechestvennykh Vostokovedov,* Vol.II, Moscow, 1995, (henceforth cited as Miliband II), p. 199
26. Information kindly sent by Prof. L.B.Alayev of Moscow
27. A.N.Shamatov, "South Asian Studies In Uzbekistan", *Journal Of Historical Studies,* Patna University, No.4, December 1998, p.101.
28. *South Asian Languages Department,* Tashkent, 1997,pp. 16-17)
29. G.M.Dmitriev, *The Indian Revolutionaries in Central Asia,* Gurgaon, 2002, Chapter entitled "Communist International And Indian Revolutionaries In Soviet Turkestan", pp. 98-130.
30. Maliev, *Hinduston Angliyaning astindah.* Tashkent, 1920.
31. Shaukat Usmani, " India and Russian Revolution III", *Mainstream,* New Delhi July 15, 1967, p.27.
32. *Byuletin presy Sred Vostoka* (hereafter cited as *Byuletin,),* Tashkent, 1928, No. 2, pp.141-175.
33. *Byuletin,* Tashkent, Nos. 1,2 and3.
34. *Bibliografia...,* p. 222, No. 2997 and p. 223, No 3998.
35. Azizov, "Na Indo-Afganskoye granitse (Vosstaniye afganskikh plemen", Na *Zarubezhnom Vostoke,* Tashkent, 1933, No 3-4 pp. 119-128. Ferestanov, D., " Britanskay voennay ekspiditsiya v polosy nezabisimikh plemen (iyul-sentyambr, 1933)", *Na Zarubezhnom Vostake.* Tashkent, 1933 No., 5, pp. 74-83.
36. Articles by Kensington and G. Mac-Munn regarding British expeditions to tribal areas were translated into Russian and published.
37. T. Scott, " Vosstaniye v Kashmire", trans, from English by D. Ferestanov, *Byul. Zarubezhnoy Voeyn-presy no Vostoky,* Tashkent, 1933, No.1, pp. 1-13. Kashkin K., "Vosstaniye v Alware", *Na Zarubezhnom Vostaoke,* Tashkent, 1933, No., 3-4, pp. 91-117.

38. "Indiya Rabochiye dvizheniye: Revolutsnoye Krestianskoye, dvizheniye", *Na Zarubezhnom Vostoke,* Tashkent, 1932, No.1, pp. 54-69)
39. "Polozheniye rabochego klassa i rabochiyee dvizheniye", *Na Zarubekhnom Vostoke,* Tashkent,1934, No.2, pp. 91-101; I.M. Reusner, "Agrarnaya programma Induskogo natsionalnogo kongresa", *Na Zarubezhnom Vostoke,* Tashkent, 1939, No.2, pp. 1-11.
40. *Bibliografia...,* p. 230, Nos. 4156, 4157.
41. *Ibid.,* Nos. 4163, 4164, 4165, 4168, 4174; p. 231, No.4183.
42. *Ibid.,* Nos. 4159 ,4166, 4170; p. 231, Nos. 4182, 4184.
43. For details of the writings of the Soviet indologists during this period see my paper, " India and Soviet Central Asia in Pre-Independence Days', *Dialogue,* Vol. 3 No.4, April-June 2002, pp.163-174
44. *The Hindu,*19 July 1954
45. G.K.Shirokov, "B.G.Gafurov I Vostokovedeniye" in M.C.Lebedev (Compiler), *V Masshtabe Veka,* Moscow, 1999, pp. 102-112.
46. Ibid.,p.110.
47. G. G. Kotovskii, "Bobojan Gafurovich Gafurov—Glava Sovetskogo Vostokovedeniya" in M.C.Lebedev, op.cit.,p.116.
48. Information supplied by Professor Qamar Rais, who has spent several years in Tashkent from 1960s onwards and had been a teacher and a Director of Indian Cultural Centre in Tashkent.
49. S.D. Miliband *Bibliograficheskii Slovar Otechestvennykh Vostokovedov*, Vol.II, Moscow,1995,102
50. Shamatov, p. 103
51. Information supplied by Prof. Azad Shamatov, a former student of Hardat and now the Head, South Asian Studies Department, Tashkent University, vide his email dated 4 / 6 / 2004.
52. M.M.Khhairullaev,P.G.Bulgakov,U.M.Ariper and I.M.Khasimov (eds), *Narodov Srednei Azii I Indii (hereafter cited as Iz Islorii kulturnykh Svyazei ...),*Tashkent,1986, p. 147.
53. A.N. Shamatov, "South Asian Studies in Uzbekistan" (henceforth cited as Shamatov), *Journal of Historical Studies,* Number 4, December 1998, p. 101. See also *South Asian Languages Department*, p.16
54. Shamatov, p. 101. See also *South Asian Languages Department*, p.16
55. Shamatov, p. 103.
56. Miliband II, p. 482.

57. L. Kharyukov, *Friendship University*, Soviet Land Booklets, New Delhi, 1991
58. Ibid., pp.83,84
59. Shamatov, p.102. See also *South Asian Languages Department*, p.8
60. B.T.Abidov and A.R.Sahibaev, "India V Trudakh Uchenykh Instituta Vostokovedeniya Akademii Nauk Uzbekistana" (cyclostyled copy), p.2
61. *Historical and Cultural Links*,p.34
62. Mliband, II, p. 574
63. A.Rajabov and V. Mirzoeva (editor-in chiefs), *Bobojon Gafurov, Investigator Of History And Culture Of Peoples From Central Asia,* Dushanbe, 1998, p.410.(Henceforth cited as *Gafurov).*
64. *Historical and Cultural Links between India & Uzbekistan* (hereafter cited as *Historical and Cultural Links* Khuda Bakhsh International Seminar, 1993, Patna, 1996, p.34
65. Ibid.,p. 34
66. Shamatov, p. 101.
67. *Iz Istorii kulturnykh...,* p. 14.
68. Miliband II, p. 318.
69. *Iz Istorii kultunykh...,* pp. 147-58.
70. Abidov and Sahibaev,p.7
71. Realism in Contemporary Indian Novels, Tashkent, 1984
72. *South Asian Languages Department*, p.22
73. Ibid.
74. Shamatov, pp. 103, 104.
75. A delegation from Bihar branch of ISCUS visited Kyrgyzia in 1987. Dr. Kumar Bimal, the eminent Hindi poet, critic and litterateur was its leader.
76. Abidov and Sahibaev, p.2
77. Miliband II, p. 523
78. M. Salye(tr), *Babur-Name,* S.A. Azimdzhanova, Editor-in-Chief, Tashkent, 1958, pp. 530; Another edition of *Babur-name* was published from Tashkent in 1982.
79. Dale, *The Garden Of The Eight Paradises,* Brill, Leiden, 2004, p. 4 f.n. 8
80. Miliband II, p. 116
81. Miliband I, p.119
82. G.L.Dmitriyev, "From the History of Indian Colony in Central Asia", in Surendra Gopal (ed) *India and Central Asia,* Delhi, 2001, p. 76

83. Biruni, *Indiya* , Tashkent, 1963
84. "Iz istorii karavannoi torgovli mezhdu Srednei Azii I Severnoi Indii v XIXv." in *Vzamootnosheniya narodov Srednei Azii i sopredelnikh stran Vostoka v XVIII—nachal XX v.*, Tashkent, 1963, pp.163-194
85. Surendra Gopal (ed) *India and Central Asia Cultural, Economic and Political Links* ,Delhi, 2002, pp.76-98.Originally the article was published in D.A.Oldderogge (chief editor), *Strany I Narody Vostoka Indiya-Strana i Narod,* kniga II, Moskva, 1972, pp.234-47
86. Sadriddin Aini, *Sobraniye Sochinenni,* Vol. V (Bukhara), Moskva,1974.Bobojon Gafurov had persuaded Aini to write his memoirs of Bukhara. The work gained immense popularity. M.S. Lebedev (Compiler), *V Mashtabe Veka*, Moskva, 1999, p.43
87. Ibid., pp.43-46
88. Nizamutdinov, pp.6-7
89. Abidov and Sahibaev, p.3
90. S.D. Miliband, *Bibliograficheskii Slovar Otechestvennykh Vostokovedov*, I , Moscow, 1995, p.532
91. Miliband II, p. 116
92. *Bibliografia...*, pp.350,351 ff.
93. B.A.Litviskii "Bobojon Gafurovich Gafurov—Osnovopolozhnik Tajikskoi Istoriicheskoi Naukoi," in *V Masshtabe Veka,* p.56
94. L.I.Miroshnikov, "Akademik B.G.Gafurov I Izucheniye Middle And Central Asia" in *V MasshtabeVeka,* pp.99-101
95. M.S. Asimov and C.E. Bosworth (eds) *History of Civilizations of Central Asia,* Volume IV, Part One, First Indian Edition, Delhi, 1999, p. 6
96. Miliband I,p.92
97. *Information Bulletin*, Issue 20, Moscow, 1994,p.156
98. Stavisky, *Sudba Buddisma V Srednei Azii*, Moscow,1998,p.165
99. *Information...*, p.160
100. Ibid.,162
101. *Sudba*, p.5
102. Gafurov, p.418
103. Dmitry Volsky, *The Developments In The Indian Subcontinent And The* Soviet *Union* (in Hindi), Delhi,1972,p.13
104. Ibid., p.7
105. A. Rajabov and V. Mizoeva (eds.), pp. 360, 361.
106. Ibid., p. 363
107. Ibid., pp. 363-64

108. Ibid., p. 367
109. Ibid.
110. Ibid., p. 368
111. Ibid., P. 369
112. Ibid., p. 370
113. Ibid., p. 370
114. Ibid., pp. 370-71
115. My English translation as "An Essay on the Ethnography of a Group of Indic Language Speaking Pariah (In The Hissar Valley)" is available in *India and Central Asia*..., pp.139-62
116. "Central Asia in Antiquity: Problems of History and Culture", in *Budushchyeye Nauki* , Moscow, 1983, pp.254-269
117. Gafurov, p. 371
118. Ibid., p. 372
119. Ibid., p. 373
120. Gafurov, B.,. "Bahr al-Asrar II", *Journal of the Pakistan Historical Society*,14/2 (1966),pp.43-50
121. For details see Richard C. Foltz, *Mughal India And Central Asia,* Oxford University Press, Karachi,1998,Chapter 6 entitled "Travelogues",pp.106-25
122. *Iz istorii*...,p.177
123. See also Supra
124. *Iz Istorii kulturnykh* ...,p.178
125. Information supplied by Prof. L.B.Alayev,who was the main organizer of Baku Conference.
126. Shail Mayaram, "Komal Kothari rooted in oral tradition", *The Hindu,* 20 June 2004
127. *Iz Istorii* kulturnykh..., p.34
128. G.L.Dmitriyev, Iz Istorii Sredneaziatsko-Indiiskikh Otnoshenii Vtoroi Poloviny Xix-Nachala XX V. (indiiskiye Vykhodtsy V Srednei Azii), Avtoreferat, Tashkent, 1965
129. G.L.Dmtriev, *Indian Revolutionaries In Central Asia*, Gurgaon, 2002
130. Abidov and Sahibaev,p.4
131. Ibid.
132. Ibid., pp.3-6
133. Mliband II, 154
134. T.K.Bishembiev, *Tarikh-i- Shahrukhi,*Alma-Ata, 1987, pp.81-83
135. M. Blagonravova, *The Youth of the USSR and India,* Novosti Press Agency publishing House, Moscow, 1974, pp43-46
136. *Is Istorii Kulturnykh*..., p. 171

137. Zafar Imam, "The Al-Beruni Library- A Live Symbol Of Indo-Uzbek Cross Culture" in *Historical and Cultural Links*, pp.426-31
138. Ata Khurseed, "Dictionaries & Grammar Books Of Uzbek (Chugtai-Turkish) Language & Other Manuscripts Preserved In Maulana Azad Library, Aligarh," in Ibid.,pp.397-408
139. Surendra Gopal, "Indian Traders in Uzbekistan in the Eighteenth Century," in *India and Central Asia* ,pp.19-43
140. *Annual Report Of The Ministry Of External Affairs, Government Of India*, New Delhi, 1992-93, p.4
141. Ibid.,1993-1994,pp.26,27

The Role of Indo-Central Asian Relations in Making a New Asia

Post–1991 Period

European colonialism, beginning in the post- Vasco da Gama period in Asia and Africa consolidated itself in the era of Industrial Revolution and reached its peak in the 19th century. Though exploitation, political, economic and cultural, was its hallmark, colonialism brought printing press which assisted an ever expanding sense of self-consciousness among the subject people. The process was helped by steam engine induced people's mobility. A new sense of identity, nationalism, grew up in the colonies. Revolutions broke out against seemingly invincible rulers. The Asian determination to oust Europeans was steeled when Japan defeated Tsarist Russia in Russo-Japanese War of 1904-05. Four decades later, after the Second World War, European colonialism was in full retreat from Asia and Africa.

The newly liberated countries, oppressed and exploited by metropolitan countries, embarked upon the path of development, social, economic and cultural. Basically the choice was between the ideologies of capitalism and communism, represented by USA and USSR respectively. An intense cold war developed between the two super powers. The 'war' ended after almost half-a-century when in 1991 the Soviet Union disintegrated. Simultaneously the newly emerging forces of globalization pushed the ideological factor in the background. The USA was the unquestioned super power in the unipolar world.

International relations had to be recast. The question of security required new thinking in the new world perspective.

Making of a Policy

New sovereign states emerged on the ruins of the Soviet Union in the eastern Europe and in the heart of the Eurasian continent from Armenia to Kyrgyzstan. They posed security problems to adjacent states including our country. Barring the Soviet regime, during the last two thousand and five hundred years, India had been repeatedly invaded by powers marching from Central Asia.

The situation was grim. India now face unprecedented problem, the foremost was the fear of the use of nuclear weapons.

The Soviet space station as well as nuclear installations were located in Kazakhstan, a newly independent state. Throughout its existence, the Soviet Union had ensured that the nuclear weapons had never been used. Even though Russia, the major successor of the Soviet Union, had taken adequate precaution to prevent the use of nuclear weapons, one could not rule out the possibility of their misuse in new hands. There were solid reasons for visualizing such a situation.

Islamic fundamentalism was rapidly growing. Libya, Iraq, Iran and Pakistan, all Islamic states, were keen to possess/acquire nuclear weapons. They had made their intentions known to the whole world. These Central Asia States had dominantly Muslim population. Their economy then was pitiable. Oil-rich Middle Eastern States could try to lure them with big money. One could not predict their behaviour in the face of such allurements. At least their nuclear scientists could be 'hired' or 'invited' to assist the programme of nuclearisation.

With the demise of the Soviet Union, the communist ideology was given a burial. The danger was that Islamic Fundamentalism could step in the ideological vacuum. In the neighbouring Afghanistan the Islamic fundamentalists, the Talibans, had obtained the upper hand. They could propagate their ideals or even forcibly try to impose them on their neighbours. They could invoke 'Islamic Brotherhood' to put across their message to the masses. (For details of the rise of Islamic fundamentalism in post-1991 Central Asia, see *Combating Religions Extremism in Central Asia : Problems and Perspective Conference Materials,*

Dushanbe, Tajikistan, April 25, 2002) India viewed this possibility with great alarm. India has around 160 million Muslims.

The emergence of a Turkish- speaking block extending from the Mediterranean to the Pamirs had to be taken into account. This could revive the moribund Pan-Turanism. A solid block of Turkish-speaking nations would alter the geo-political situation and India had to cope with this problem.

Finally, India visualized a far more serious problem. Pakistan, India's immediate neighbour and initiator of four wars during the last four decades was posing itself as the trustworthy friend of the newly independent Central Asian States only on the basis of commonality of religion. Pakistan had been an active member of USA-Sponsored Defense Pacts and Military Blocs. These military alliances, directed against the Soviets had been then denounced by the Soviet Union. The Central Asians, then a part of the Soviet Union, had more or less, shunned Pakistan. Pakistan thought that the death of the Soviet Union gave it a new opportunity to draw them within its own sphere of influence.

India had to prevent such a development because of its continuing adversarial relationship with Pakistan which seldom lost any opportunity to show its hostility.

These facts must have been in the mind of Indian policy makers; their immediate concern was to prevent neuclearisation of the area, ensure non-proliferation of nuclear weapons, and to keep the new sovereign states away from the ideologies of Pan Turanism and Pan Islamism. They had to ensure that Pakistan did not develop a cosy relation with them. India could hope success as some favourable factors were operating.

Helpful Factors

First, the Central Asian countries as sovereign nation states were still closely allied to Russia both economically and politically because of compulsions of history and geography. The presence of Russia was a guarantee that nuclear weapons would not fall into the hands of non-nuclear Central Asian states. Super power USA and 'big' neighbour China were also in favour of non-nuclearisation of Central Asian states. India, Russia, USA and China all supported nuclear *status quo*.

The Central Asian states had been nurtured on a philosophy of atheism for seven decades; it was expected that the people would not be easily taken in by fundamentalist Islamic propaganda. The belief was justified although Tajikistan proved to be an exception. It had plunged into a civil war as soon as the Soviet power collapsed.[1] Steeped in secular and scientific education, people were more receptive to the voice of nationalism than to the tenets of fundamental Islam.

Indian policy makers after weighing the pros and cons of the situation decided to take advantage of these positive points; they set about forging a mutually beneficial relationship which would be keen on promoting liberal and democratic values and helping market economic forces to emerge in tune with forces of globalisation.

India's formulation of the new policy was right. Luckily for India the two important immediate neighbours, Russia and China the two largest countries in Euro-Asia did not feel their strategic or economic interests were threatened by Indian initiative.

India's initial policy moves were halting and hesitant as compared to Pakistan because India tried to ensure they were in harmony with Russian sensibilities and did not fan Chinese fears.

India's foreign policy incorporated new factors and took initiative to serve India's interests better as time progressed. For Indian authorities matters were made somewhat easier by the fact that the change of regimes had not meant a change of government except in Tajikistan. In Turkmenistan, Uzbekistan, Kyrgyzstan and Kazakhstan, the old government wedded to secularism, with a pro-Russian tilt remained in power. Many in India government were well acquainted with these leaders. The Indian policy makers took advantage of this and unfolded steps to convince these states of usefulness of continuing traditional friendship of the Soviet era with India.

First, the region, a geographical entity, consisted of countries of diverse size, resources and perception of security and foreign policy interests. No foreign policy could ignore there differences and India was no exception.

India realized that the new states were rich in energy resources, petrol and gas. A mutually beneficial relation would help to solve India's chronic deficiency in these products. "Caspian basin held huge reserves which were waiting to be intensively exploited. According to an estimate (*International Petroleum Encyclopaedia 1998*,Oaklahoma, USA) Turkestan has between 17 and three trillion cubic metres of untapped gas, estimated to be world's second largest reserve. Other Central Asian Republics together have oil and gas equivalent to that of Qatar, Oman and UAE, put together. They can produce seven million barrels of oil daily, but for the huge investments required."[2] India as one of the largest consumer of hydrocarbons was keen to benefit from the new source of supplies.

Uzbekistan at the heart of Central Asia, is the largest populated state had more cultivable land than the rest of the States except Kazakhstan. Its mineral resources were enormous. Besides petroleum and gas, it was fifth in gold stock and seventh in its production in the world. It was fifth in cotton production in the world. The tradition of monoculture, i.e. cultivating only cotton in the Soviet times had made it deficient in food grains.

Uzbekistan had more industries and traditionally it was more urbanized and had better facilities for higher education.[3] It was quickly given diplomatic recognition and today is recognized by 170 countries.[4] On the other hand Kazakhstan had a large percentage of Russian population. In the Soviet times, Russia had created facilities for launching its space vehicles and storing nuclear weapons on its soil. Russia was afraid that these nuclear arms would fall into alien hands and jeopardize its security. Therefore, it carefully controlled the foreign policy of Kazakhstan.

Turkmenistan had discovered enormous quantities of oil and gas. It was also a corridor to Central and Southern Europe for the neighbouring Central Asian States. Its foreign policy aimed at ensuring its neutrality from the entanglements in which the other Central Asian States found themselves.

Hence, the Indian government while formulating its policies had to consider Central Asia as a unit and at the same time it could not forget the individual concerns of each country as well. It had also to compete with neighbours like Pakistan who invoked solidarity in the name of religion and/or language/or geography.

For example, in 1999, Pakistani missionaries in Kyrgyzstan numbered forty and were the second largest group of foreign missionaries.

Islam Karimov had mentioned that they had the largest reserves of gas and petroleum and 'the world cannot forget it.'

Unfolding of the Policy

India's relationship with Central Asia in Soviet times was only cultural and economic; now they had to be reinforced with diplomacy as the security of India was involved. Pakistan , having tasted success in Afghanistan in ousting the Soviets, opted for an aggressive foreign policy in the region; it projected itself as the true friend of Central Asian States and was not averse to play the Islamic card in the name of Pan Islamism. Though Pakistan had nothing to offer in economic terms, it sought to grant them access to the Arabian Sea through the port of Karachi or other ports on the Makran coast. It also played upon Central Asia's historic fear of Shia Iran and was offering the land-locked States an access to sea bypassing Iran. Pakistan also sought to put forward itself as a long-standing friend of the People's Republic of China their next-door neighbour. It claimed it could keep China in good humour which would benefit the Central Asian States as the Soviet shield had been withdrawn.

Pakistan's agenda in dominating Afghanistan and the newly independent Central Asian States was to ensure the so-called doctrine of 'strategic depth.'

Of course the Central Asian States had their own problems. Tajikistan was confronted with a civil war immediately after it became independent. *Mujahdins* from Afghanistan threatened it. The security of national frontiers against Afghan invaders was its first concern.

The small Kyrgyzstan was self-sufficient in food and dairy products.[5]

Forging of mutual trust and respect for each other's interest was a *sine qua non* for a durable and fruitful relationship and the Indian government set about the task with determination. India had no problem in formally establishing diplomatic relations with the newly established countries though in certain cases there was a small time lag before the embassies could be established. India took six years to open an embassy in Dushanbe (Tajikistan).

Establishment of relationship with Uzbekistan was the easiest. India had a diplomatic presence in Tashkent during the Soviet days. The office was upgraded and Tashkent became the pivot round which India's diplomatic activities took place in other Central Asian republics. In Uzbeksitan India had a small economic presence towards the last days of the Soviet Union. The Tata and L.& T. group of Companies were constructing Hotels in 1990 in Tashkent and Samarkand—the capital of Timurid Uzbekistan. Indians were permitted to expand to expand their economic activities and allowed to set up new industries.

Indians started pharmaceutical companies in Uzbekistan.[6] In 2000, the turn over of trade amounted to $25.3 million.[7]

India's intense desire to obtain gas and petroleum, the two products available in plenty in the Central Asian States was not lost upon these nations. They were conscious that new economic ties should be accompanied by close political relationship between the Central Asian States and India.

The Uzbek President Karimov promptly responded. His first visit to India took place in August 1991. He followed it with visits in 1994 and 2000.[8]

Indian Prime Minister P. V. Narasimha Rao reciprocated and visited Uzbekistan in 1993 and spelled out Indian concerns especially in relation to the growth of religious extremism. At the same time he pledged support to the legitimate interests of the newly independent country.

From now on exchange of visits at different levels between Central Asian States and India commenced. Attempts were initiated to establish mutually satisfying relationships, cultural, economic and political.

The above Indo-Central Asian interactions have to be seen in context of Pakistani policies in the region.

Pakistan

While India was expanding its relations quietly, Pakistan

was more aggressive; it was trying hard to woo the Central Asian States and bring them within its orbit of influence. It was in a better position to influence the course of events in Central Asia because of its alliance with the ruling faction in Afghanistan. Pakistan's effort was directed at preventing close Indo-Central Asian relations. In 1995 Ms. Bhutto, the Pakistan Prime Minister went to Uzbekistan and almost immediately Saudi Arabia agreed to set up a joint venture worth $ 31 million. They wanted Uzbekistan to toe their policies. Uzbekistan, however, did not commit.[9] Pakistan's President Farooq Ahmad Khan Leghari in October 1996 visited Bishkek and promised to link Kazakhstan and Kyrgyzstan with the Karakoram highway so that their dependence on other Central Asian States for access to the outside world would be reduced. He also asked them to use the port of Karachi rather than Bander Abbas in Iran to reach the sea as it would be a shorter path.

To lure the Central Asian States to join the Islamic Bloc, economic allurements were put forward. A delegation of Islamic Development Bank based in Jidda visited Turkmenistan, Uzbekistan , Kazakhstan, etc. in 1996 but not much came out of it. Kazakhstan would not be persuaded. It had applied for membership of the North-South-Sea- Road corridor running through Iran.

Politically India and the Central Asian states started coming nearer after the latter realized that the Chechen rebels, Talibans and Pakistanis were keen to stir up internal dissension in the name of establishing Islamic polity.

Meanwhile India had begun an exercise to reach Central Asian States bypassing Pakistan and Afghanistan. India received full support from Iran, disenchanted with internal developments in Afghanistan. The former, like India, was keen to develop friendly relations with Central Asian States and was, therefore, willing to co-operate with India, in its endeavour to overcome geographical obstacles. Geography had been a major hindrance to the development of closer economic relations between India and Central Asian States as they are separated by intervening states and do not have direct access to each other. These intervening states had their own agenda and were unwilling to see flourishing economic relations between these two regions. However both sides showed keenness to overcome this geographical barrier. The idea of developing the North-South-Sea-Road corridor from Bander Abbas in Iran to Anzali and then to the Caspian port of Astrakhan was floated and was being vigorously pursued. Indo-Iran understanding made this project a reality; Central Asian states could reach Arab Sea and India and access the Caspian Sea without going to Pakistan and Afghanistan. The Central Asian States, under economic compulsions were overcoming their traditional distrust of Shiite Iran because the unhindered access to the Persian Gulf opened up for them vast markets on the rim of the Indian Ocean where competition was less and the likelihood of economic gain was far greater than either in Europe or in China. Russia, so long their major purchaser and supplier, was restructuring its economy and was in no position to serve their immediate interests.

The Central Asian Republics were convinced of Pakistan's close links with religious extremism, terrorism and Talibans after the Islamic movement of Uzbekistan made a bid to stir trouble in Uzbekistan, Tajikistan and Kyrgyzstan in 1999. It is reported that 30 Kyrgyz soldiers lost their lives[10] Uzbekistan had taken a little more time than other republics to reach this conclusion.

The Central Asian States were disenchanted by the pro-Taliban policies, pursued by Pakistan.

Pakistan attempted to join Shanghai Five Grouping formed by Russia, Kazakhstan, Kyrgyzstan , Tajikistan and China in 1996 in face of mounting threat from Afghan fundamentalists. China was deeply concerned at the trouble it was facing at the hands of the religious fundamentalists and terrorists in its western-most province of Xinjiang, bordering both Afghanistan and Pakistan. It had promoted the Shanghai Five Group.[11]

The Chinese were friendly but noncommittal. The Chinese Foreign Ministry spokesman said, "but, I think, taking new members requires negotiated consensus of the five members of the Shanghai Five". The application was submitted to 'Group's current Chair, Tajikistan'.[12] But the Russian Foreign Ministry emphatically ruled out Pakistan's request. Its spokesman asserted, "it is a pure propaganda move".[13]

Uzbekistan was earlier lukewarm to the Group of Shanghai Five; it adopted a neutral position on the question of opposing and fighting growing Islamic fundamentalism along its border.

At a conference in 1996 convened in Tehran to chalk out a strategy to meet the threat being posed by the Talibanisation in Afghanistan, Uzbekistan abstained while Iran, Russia, India and four Central Asian States attended it.[14] Uzbekistan's reluctance to clearly spell out its stand against terrorism, prompted the three states Kyrgyzstan, Kazakhstan and Tajikistan to seek support elsewhere. They found close allies in both Russia and China. The former was already suffering at the hands of Chechen rebels.

In early 1998 Uzbek Foreign Minister Abdulaziz Kamilov accused Islamabad of giving military training to Uzbek rebels. He said the some 400 Kyrgyz, Tajik and Uzbek rebels were undergoing training at illegal camps in Pakistan. He also accused the rebels, trained in Pakistan of a series of attacks in Uzbekistan's Namagan region last year which led to the deaths of several government employees and law officers. The Pakistan government vehemently denied these charges.[15] But it was clear that Pakistan's bid to draw Uzbekistan in its orbit had failed.

The year 1999 proved to be a defining moment. Certain events forced the governments of Uzbekistan and Kyrgyzstan to shed their inhibitions and to commit their support to the ongoing struggle against religious fundamentalism and international terrorism. A major aim of the foreign policies of India and Central Asian States was the same. The Central Asian States corrected their pro-Pakistani tilt. In the international arena India and Central Asian States were coming together.

Uzbekistan had to change its stand when the Islamic fundamentalists tried to stir up trouble in Tashkent and caused a series of blasts in the capital. An attempt was made to assassinate President Islam Karimov on 16 February 1999. It was clear that the Islamic Movement of Uzbekistan (IMU) led by Namangani which had intruded into the Ferghana Valley had well-established links with the Taliban. At a later date, in August 1999, armed bands entered Kyrgyzstan and the government forces had difficulty in putting them down. Some of the members of these armed bands also entered Uzbekistan and tried to create trouble. The Uzbek government was forced to bomb the guerilla's stronghold.

In July 1999 in Delhi Prime Minister Vajpayee had 'made a plea to the peoples of South Asia and Central Asia for taking the only possible route of "Peace, friendship and cooperation among the countries of the region". He described the people of the area as a "geocultural family of which we were, and continue to be members".[16] Nareshwar Dayal Secretary (East) Ministry of External Affairs on that occasion stressed the "Positive determinants of Indo-Central Asian Relations". These were the 'need to build roads and railway; pipelines would have to be laid to transport energy resources of South Asia; thus overcoming the access to the land-locked Central Asia".[17] Apparently the Pakistan's nuclear test of 1998 alerted him to the danger posed by a nuclearized Pakistan supported by terrorists and fundamentalists. Such position undoubtedly brought India and Uzbekistan and other Central Asian States together. In March 2000, Islam Karimov visited India and the Indo-Uzbekistan Joint economic Commission intensified its activities and to date has held four sittings.[18]

Meanwhile to ensure their security as a follow up measure, in May 2001 a decision was taken to create a rapid-reaction force consisting of a battalion 'from each of the four participants Russia, Kyrgyzstan, Tajikistan, and Kazakhstan'. The force was to be subordinate to a 'joint headquarters based in Kyrgyzia'.[19] A statement added, "We will continue to jointly rebuff attempts to rebuff peace and tranquility in Central Asia,..." Russia had also sought and secured the support of CIS nations in its fight against religious fundamentalism and terrorism.

After Uzbekistan had hardened its stance against terrorism, at a meeting of the Shanghai Five in June 2001, it was admitted as a founder – member of Shanghai Cooperation Organisation.[20] This showed that these countries were fully 'aware of the Taliban-led extremist links in their countries' and were determined that 'the problem of religions extremism, and terrorism be effectively controlled'.[21]

The turn of events in Afghanistan showed that the Talibans were keen to export their brand of Islamic fundamentalism and to establish *Nizam-i-Millat,* the Republic of Islamic fundamentalism stretching from the borders of India to deep into the Volga country of Russia and Chechnya and Tatarstan. Hence, the small Central Asian States had no option but to turn to democratic countries opposed to fundamentalism and this brought a better appreciation for India's bold stand against terrorism.

Uzbek scholars were forthright in assessing the role of India in fighting terrorism and religious extremism. Muhammad M. Yukbov of the Institute of Strategic and Regional Studies of Uzbekistan stated, "India is quite experienced in handling fundamentalism and religious extremism, and since we are faced with almost identical problems, we will be glad to have the benefit of its knowledge.'[22] His colleagues Abdullah Zia Abdullaev and Isadjanov agreed with him and suggested that India, Uzbekistan and other countries of the region should co-operate and evolve a mechanism to fight fundamentalism and religious extremism. [23]

The Uzbek appreciation of India's position certainly influenced other Central Asian States' policies towards India and this was reflected in visits of Heads of States of Central Asia to India in 2001.

The leadership of Central Asian States was deeply affected by the events which took place in Uzbekistan and Kyrgyzstan in July and August 1999, when armed bands (members of Islamic Movement of Uzbekistan) entered from Tajikistan into Uzbekistan and Kyrgyzstan and the government struggled hard to suppress the terrorists. The rebels were supported by Laden and they were planning to set up bases in the mountains to stir up further troubles.[24]

The experience impelled the two governments, of Uzbekistan and Kyrgyzstan, to take a definite stand against terrorism and religious extremism and this brought them near to the Indian position.

Earlier the rebels had imprisoned four Japanese geologists and German mountaineers and several others in Kyrgyzstan. They were released only after a hefty ransom was paid.

The foreign governments, especially the European Union countries, who were investing in the Central Asian States were worried about the growing instability in the region. The Central Asian States were nervous that this would affect Foreign Investment and would have a deleterious impact on their economy in the long run.

Pakistan made another desperate attempt to rope in Central Asian States to its side.

In November 2000, Pakistan's Chief Executive went on a two-day visit to Kazakhstan.[25] En route he met Turkmenistan's President Saparmurat Niazaov during a brief stop over do discuss Afghanistan. This was the third meeting of President Nursultan Nazarbayev with Gen. Musharraff during the year. The aim was to remove Kazakhstan's perception that Pakistan 'is in hand in glove with the Taliban regime in Afghanistan...' and this was to enhance political and economic relations with the Central Asian Republics. Central Asian States were in no doubt that India and not the Islamic Pakistan was their true friend.

To terrorise the Tajiks, the Talibans moved 1,000 gunmen to Tolukan border region, close to the Tajik international line but the Russians stationed there felt they could repel any attempted intrusion on part of the Talibans.[26] Even the Chinese in Western Xinjiang bordering on Tajikistan, Kyrgyzstan, Kazakhstan and Afghanistan, were feeling the heat of Talibanism and Wanabism and were deeply concerned since Xinjiang was their gateway to capital Urumqi and Kazakhstan. The border trade with Kyrgyzstan via the Turgurt pass was too invaluable to be lost to fundamentalists. Hence, China extended its support to Central Asian States for eliminating terrorism.[27]

Within less than a decade, Russia, the Central Asian States and China had all suffered from the ravages caused by the Talibans and the proponents of similar ideologies, both at home and abroad.

The experience impelled the two governments to take a decisive stand against terrorism and extremism. This brought them near to the Indian position. The Tajik President Imam Ali Rakhmanov came to India on a four-day visit in May 2001.[28] Rakhmanov's worries were understandable. It is a frontline state and gateway for the Talibans to the Farghana Valley, i.e. both Uzbekistan and Kyrgyzstan. Russia realizing the predicament of Tajikistan stationed 30,000 troops to deter Taliban armed bands from crossing into Tajikistan.[29] During Tajik President's visit, India pledged support to Tajikistan and agreed to set up food processing industries. Certainly Tajikistan's conduct in restoring their reclining 42 ft. long and 9ft. high Buddha found in 1960 brought to Indians their secular credential, especially in the aftermath of the destruction of the Bamian Buddhas by the Talibans. It was no surprise that the Indian government supported the Tajik government which had endured civil war and political unrest through most of the 1990s.[30] A clear statement of their solidarity in fight against terrorism and religious extremism was made.

The Indo-Tajik declaration signed during the Tajik President Emomali Sharifovik Rakhmanov visit in May 2001 covered the 'entire gamut of bilateral ties as well as regional and international issues of mutual concern'.[31] India offered a grant of five million US dollars to Tajikistan to tackle the acute drought situation and five agreements were concluded such as one on economic co-operation and another for joint action against terrorism and drug trafficking.[32] The Tajik President offered to support India's candidacy for a permanent seat on the Security Council.

The clear formulation of a policy of resistance to the spread of religious extremism and terrorism by Shanghai Five and Uzbekistan encouraged the Northern Alliance which was battling the Talibans to send its Foreign Minister Abdulla to Moscow in July 2001 to ' build up international pressure to rein in the Taliban'.[33]

When the events of 11 September 2001 took place in new York, the Central Asian States, Russia, China, India and Northern Alliance were already bound to support each other against religious extremists and terrorists.

More importantly, USA assumed the leadership of international efforts to contain, and wipe out terrorism by formulating the 'Doctrine of War on Terror.' China also lent its unqualified support. In persuit of this aim USA jumped into war against the Talibans in Afghanistan (considered to be the fountain-head of Islamic terrorism) and sought and received military bases in Central Asian States. When the USA decided to launch air strike against the Taliban positions in Afghanistan, Uzbekistan offered them the use of Tuzel Military Base situated not far from Tashkent.[34] The Kyrgyz Parliament permitted USA to set up a military base at Manas International Air Port, 30 kms away from capital Bishkek. Tajikistan offered three airfields, Kulyab, Khojent and Kurgam-Tyube to USA.

Indian foreign policy had consistently advocated the creation of a unified front against terrorism; it was fully vindicated; India and Central Asia found a common language; soon they agreed to widen the areas of their co-operation.

The coming together of India and Central Asian States was a rebuff to Pakistan, always keen to drive a wedge between the two. Success, however, was tinged with new anxieties. India worried about proliferation of American military bases. Pakistan after American victory over the Talibans in Afghanistan changed sides, came over to Americans. Pakistan's shadow loomed over India's policy towards Central Asian states. Nevertheless Indian policy showed a new dynamism; it developed multidimensional relationship with new states.

The post-9/11 period witnessed a new direction to the foreign policies of India and the Central Asian States. Terrorism had bared its fangs and the whole world recognized its unsavoury character. The threat posed by it had to be met unitedly.

The Central Asian Republics and India decided to upgrade their economic relations by ensuring easier access to the markets of both the areas. Since Afghanistan had been freed from the control of the Talibans by an international military action, the political scenario had changed. Pakistan had allowed international forces free access to its territory and its government had openly denounced terrorism and fundamentalism and agreed to support the new government in Afghanistan. Afghanistan and Pakistan both agreed to serve as a new link between the Central Asian

States and littoral countries of the Arabian Sea. India and Iran decided to open new routes to Central Asian States via Afghanistan.

The port of Chabahar on Iran's Makran coast close to Pakistani port of Gwadar in Baluchistan province was selected as a new terminal port. A road is being built which would enter Afghanistan in the province of Heart and it would go on to Termez on the Oxus river in Uzbekistan.

Pakistan aware of the changed mood of international politics is reorienting its policy. It withdrew support to Talibans and al-Qaeda and pledged its support in suppressing terrorism. It agreed to prevent nuclear proliferation by stopping supply or sale of nuclear parts to Libya, Iran and North Korea. It now reoriented its policy towards India. By establishing its credentials as an anti-terrorist state, as a believer in non-nuclear proliferation, and a champion of regional co-operation, Pakistan put itself forward as a transit point for road-link between India and Uzbekistan. It showed keenness that gas pipelines from Iran and Central Asia to India should run through it because it would bring immense economic benefit to it and also will be economically viable for India.

India carefully assessed the moves of Pakistan; the Central Asian states also felt that the shorter route through Pakistan to India and other countries of South Asia would promote their economy as well.

Meanwhile, India continuously strengthened its relationship with Central Asian states through diplomacy, intensified educational and cultural relations.

For example, Indian cultural centers were opened in Tashkent (Uzbekistan) and Almaty (Kazakhstan) with Vinode Bhatia and Naseem Bhatia as Directors respectively. Both of them were familiar with the Soviet system and fluent in Russian as they had studied for their Ph.D. degrees in Moscow.

Besides, the Indian Government established at the University of World Economics and Diplomacy in Tashkent and at the University of Osh in Kyrgyzstan one Chair each, to teach "Indian Civilization-study in Continuity and Change: Unity in Diversity". Indian scholars were appointed to these Universities.[35]

Indian diplomacy became more active after the shock administered to it by terrorist attack on Indian Parliament on 13 December 2001.

The event alerted the Central Asian states as well as USA to the scourge of terrorism with its philosophy to spare none of its opponents. Democratic nations had to close their ranks and fight it world-wide.

Central Asian nations shed their hesitancy and resolved firmly to confront the menace. China too openly came out in support of anti-terrorist block. It agreed to collaborate actively with Russia, USA, India and Central Asian states against 'terrorism and fundamentalism'. The Central Asian State also forgot their traditional hostility to Iran. For the first time regional and world powers had combined to confront terrorism; their major target was extinction of Taliban power in Afghanistan. Even Pakistan, the most reliable Taliban ally, changed its stance and came over to the side of USA. But Pakistan's intentions still remained suspect though its disassociation with the Talibans was welcomed. The distrust of Pakistan was evinced in attempts to join Central Asia with the Arabian Sea bypassing Pakistan. This was reflected in establishing the port Chabahar on the Iranian coast and to connect it with the road net work of Afghanistan running to the Oxus river via Herat. The policy of active opposition to terrorism once again brought the Central Asian States and India together. The port of Chabahar symbolized the new policy. From now onwards the focus of policies of India and Central Asian States was to ensure a terror-free region. They had full support of Russia, China and USA and European nations.

Policy in the Post-9/11 Period

In this period two considerations have been uppermost; militarisation of the area to crush terrorism and to deter terrorists and to promote economic development so as to prevent unemployed local youths from swelling the ranks of terrorists out of frustration. USA and Russia acquired military bases and stationed their troops. The armies of Central Asian states were reorganized; they were trained and equipped to fight terrorists and secessionists. India also helped in the recognisation of the armies of Central Asian states by supplying arms and organizing training programmes. Of course, this was nowhere near to the efforts of either USA or Russia but it signified India's determination to stand by the Central Asian States.

India's visibility in the economy of the Central Asian States improved in spite of lack of direct accessibility. Indian capitalists and entrepreneurs appeared; they invested in the energy and other sectors of the economy; the most notable Indian investor is L.N. Mittal who is running a Steel Mill in Kazakhstan. Mittal has been ranked as the third richest man in the world by Forbes magazine. Simultaneously the Indian government took steps to promote close cooperation in educational and cultural spheres.

For this purpose, Indian Prime Minister and other members of Cabinet travelled to Central Asia. Similarly, Central Asian authorities regularly came over to India and have established contacts with their Indian counterparts.

Indian policy managed to keep the Central Asian States away from Pakistan, now a part of anti-terrorist alliance.

When the Americans along with their allies took up the task of driving out the Taliban from Afghanistan, India supported the military action, though it did not commit its armed forces to participate in fighting. India already had a medical mission in Tajikistan to extend medical assistance to Tajiks fighting Talibans in Afghanistan. India also committed its resources for rebuilding Afghanistan, already devastated by decades of fighting and Taliban's oppression. This was to show Central Asian States India's goodwill towards its neighbours and also its technological capabilities.

In 2002 Prime Minister Vajpayee travelled to Central Asia to gather support for India's stand.

Iran and India actively followed the policy of opening up alternative routes to Central Asia and Afghanistan with the intention of overcoming 'Pakistan barrier'.[36]

The decision to develop Chabahar port was top on India's and Iran's agenda. Iran's President Khatami was invited to India during the Republic Day parade on 26 January 2003 as the Chief

Guest. Khatami was also clear in mind that Iran was the natural gateway between Eurasia and Indian Ocean littoral.

Indian and Iranian perception about the energy resources of Central Asia coincided. Both believed that Central Asian gas and petroleum should be exported through Iran and the Arabian sea to reduce South Asian and Southeast Asian dependence on Middle Eastern oil. They could therefore, act in tandem.

India's moves on deepening Indo-Iranian relation with a view to strengthen its position *vis-a –vis* Central Asia states became clear when the Iranian President publicly announced, "Iran welcomes the presence of India in scientific and commercial fields in Central Asia". (*Hindu,* 26-1-2003). President Khatami had in 2002 visited Central Asia and was keen to have a share of Caspian oil wealth and was concerned at the growing military profile of USA in Central Asia.

An Indian delegation had visited Kazakhstan in October 2002 after Vajpayee's trip in June 2002 and held talks about Kurmangazy oil fields in the Caspian. [37]

India had given a clear idea of its intentions to have a finger in oil-pie when Punj- Lloyd of New Delhi won a stake in the Baten V. Ceyhan oil-pipeline running from Caspian to Ceyhan in Turkey.[38]

While India and Central Asia were coming closer, India did not fail to take into account the new ground situation in the Central Asian States. It was concerned at the establishment of American military bases in Central Asia. It decided to take fresh initiative and started wooing Central Asian states, especially Tajikistan where there was no American soldier and where Indian government had sent doctors to render medical aid since northern Alliance had began its fight with the Talibans.

Fear of terrorism and fundamentalism was so paramount that Shanghai group readied itself for 'regional security' by pooling their armed forces. This was the result of continuing failure of the Afghan government and the Allied forces to clear Afghanistan of Al-Qaeda elements who off and on continued to create trouble with the result that Hamid Karzai, the Afghan President was described as 'Mayor of Kabul'.

Furthermore, Pakistan's inability to control Al-Qaeda remanants caused more anxiety in the area.

It was against this context, India continued enlarging its contacts with Central Asian states.

As a part of this strategy, Indian Prime Minister paid a visit to Beijing from 22 to 26 June 2003. this was the first visit by an Indian Prime Minister after ten years.[39] The Chinese ambassador to India Hua Junduo wrote on the occasion that the countries were 'partners and rivals'.

The need to stand up against terrorism had united the two sides.

India's resolve to promote an Indo-Iran-Central Asian understanding also took in consideration China's growing involvement in the security and economy of Central Asian states. In December 2002, China signed with Kazakhstan "Good Neighbourly Treaty of Friendship and Cooperation".[40]

In 2002, India was mainly concerned to offset the growing influence of America, Russia and China in strategic and economic matters in Central Asia. In this task, India and Iran were acting together since both were concerned at the growing military might of great powers. India and Iran looked with grave concern at the growing militarisation of Central Asian states unleashed by big powers, two of them Russia and China, their neighbours and the third USA, though situated far away had the potentiality to intervene because of the superiority of its military technology.

India's concern were manifested in steps Indian diplomacy started taking since the dawn of 2003.

First, India's Defence Minister George Fernandes decided to visit China. This was to[41] be the first by an Indian Defence Minister in decades.

The Indian Foreign Minister, Yashwant Sinha went to Kyrgystan and Tajikstan and on return travelled through Almaty where he made the statement, "we are not in Central Asia to replace anyone. We see Central Asia as part of India's extended neighbourhood and our presence there is to promote a mutually inclusive relationship."[42]

This was also the first occasion when an India foreign Minister has visited Dushanbe, the capital of Tajikistan; he pledged India's help in building roads and developing hydropower.

A meeting of official of India and Kazakhstan took place in June 2003. From Kazakhstan, D. Sathojin and from India Lt. General Shantanou Choudhary took part in an exercise to share intelligence. They affirmed that the two sides were 'together on the issue of terrorism.'[43]

In November 2003 Premier Minister Vajpayee traveled to Dushabe, the first Indian Prime Minister to do so. The two sides agreed that both were keen to see stability in the region. They also felt that there was a vast potentiality of co-operation between the two sides especially in developing hydropower and mineral resources and many other fields. It must be noted that Tajikistan has silver mines.[44]

India and Central Asian states mooted widening of military co-operation. It was argued, "About 70 per cent of the equipment with Indian armed forces is of Soviet/Russian origin and nearly 100 per cent of that has commonality with what is used in the five Central Asian States." This facilitated establishment and expansion of military cooperation. India decided to station some aircraft at the Farkhor military base in Tajikistan. Indian engineers were brought in to strengthen the runway, aircraft pens and other facilities.

The Farkhor base, also known as Ayni base, just 10 kms. away from the Tajik capital, is the first Indian military base in foreign lands.[45]

India has been going all out to develop friendly relations with all the Central Asian States to wean them away from terrorist influences and make them a part of a broad-based coalition against terrorism. India had resorted to active diplomacy along with other measures.

India's External Affairs Minister, Yashwant Sinha paid a visit to Tashkent and reiterated India's close ties with Uzbekistan.

Among other measures India was trying to develop intensive educational and cultural contacts with Central Asia states. It was carrying forward the legacy of the Soviet days with one vital difference.

Prior to 1991, Indians students and researchers went to Central Asian institutions of higher studies and learning but now the flow was reversed. Central Asian students were offered Government of India scholarships to come and study Information Technology, Management, English Language and other subjects for which they did not have suitable facilities at home. India also invited professionals from Central Asia to attend training programmes, work-shops, seminars, symposia, conferences and field-studies, etc. India also established chairs in educational institutions in Tashkent and Bishkek. Prof. Amin and Prof. Barun De have held this chair in Tashkent in the past. Another Professor of History from Delhi University is currently occupying this chair. India has forged intellectual bonds with academics of Central Asian states.

There have been regular exchange of visits by cultural troupes and sports-persons. More importantly, India has established cultural centers at Tashkent and Almaty where teaching is imparted in classical Indian music, dance and languages. Lectures and Exhibitions are organized on topics of mutual interest to India and the host country.

Indian films were shown at Film Festivals, held in Tashkent in 1992 and 1997 and at Samarkand in 1997 and 1999.[46]

Undoubtedly, the emphasis is to promote understanding between the peoples of the two countries so that government policies are approved by the locals.

Indian policy makers have to work within certain constraints, specific to the region and also emerging out of international political scenario.

It may however be pointed out that the task has now become extremely complicated because of the presence of USA armed forces in this area and also its recent decision to give Pakistan the status of a Major Non-NATO Ally This would upgrade Pakistan's military strength and affect India's security. In that case should India be not wary of the motives of both USA and Pakistan? As a counter measure, will it be in India's interest to lend support to the Russian concept of 'Russia, China, India triangle '? Indian will probably decide its course on the turn of events in the region and the international arena.

India's effort to have a share in Central Asian Energy resources may not remain a strong motivation in foreign policy formulation since accessing them economically is not feasible.

India faces another problem in establishing close relations. Given her democratic tradition , how much nearer India can get to the Central Asian States where the Heads of the State are unwilling to quit the seats of power?

Rakhmanov, the Tajik President has secured popular mandate for two 7 years term after the completion of his assignment in 2006.[47]

In 2002 the Uzbek electorate permitted Presiden Islam Karimov to run for two seven-year terms when he present term is over in 2005.[48]

In 1999, Suparmurad Niyazov, the Turkmenistan President, got a mandate to remain in office till his death.

In Azebaijan, after the death of the President, his son Aliyev won the Presidency.[49]

This is an important constraint before Indian policy makers in formulating a long term viable foreign policy towards the Central Asian States. Meanwhile our interests on several counts converge. We are together in our fight against terrorism and Islamic fundamentalism. We can help each other in developing respective economics. We shall keep coming together.

If India and Central Asia can coordinate their efforts and bypass Pakistan, 'an unreliable ally', probably the fate of Asia can be changed. The land from Caspian to the Pamirs can become economically prosperous and forward-looking territory.

Footnotes

1. Kurbonali Muhabbatov, "Religious oppositional groups in Tadjikistan : Hizb ut Tahrir" in *Combating Religious Extremism ...*, pp. 61-72; *Musulmanskiye Didery : Sotsialnaya rol I avtoritet,* Dushanbe, 2003
2. *The Times of India,23/9/2000*
3. Aloke Raj, *Uzbekistan Gantantra,Kamyabi Ka Safanama* (in Hindi), Patna, 2001,pp.8-9
4. Aloke Raj,p.17
5. *Central Asian Quarterly*, Vol.3 No.4,1996,p23

6. Alok Raj,p.5
7. *The Hindu,*31/8/2001
8. *The Hindu,30 August2001*
9. *The Hindu,* 23 November 1995
10. *Asian Age*, 9 February 2001
11. *The Hindu*, 29/4/2001
12. *The Hindu* 5 January 2001
13. *The Hindu* 6/1/2001
14. *The Central Asian Quarterly* Vol. 3, No. 4,1996,p.5
15. *The Times of India,* 19.2.1998
16. *Contemporary Central Asia,* Vol III, No.1, 1999
17. Ibid., pp.1-2
18. Aloke Raj, p.2
19. *The Hindu* ,26/5/2001
20. *The Hindu,*15/6/2001
21. *The Hindu,*15/6/2001
22. *The Hindu,* 17/7/200
23. Ibid.
24. *The Hindu,* 12/8/2000
25. *The Hindu,* Nov. 2000
26. *The Hindu,*6/9/2001
27. *The Hindu,* 11.9.2000
28. *The Hindu,*29/4/2001
29. *The Hindu,*29/4/2001
30. *The Times of India,*15/2/2001
31. *The Hindu,*11/5/2001
32. *The Hindu,* 11/5/2001
33. *The Hindu,i1/7/2001*
34. *The Hindu, 26/10/2001*
35. Information supplied by Ms. Urmil Rawal, Sr. Programme Director, (ICC & C), vide her letter No. ICC/ Mis./ 2002-03 lated 26 November, 2002
36. *The Hindu*, 3 Feb. 2003
37. *The Hindu,* 21-10-2002
38. *The Hindu,* 7/11/2002
39. *The Hindu,* 11/6/2003
40. *The Hindu,* 25/12/2002
41. *The Hindu,* 27/1/2003
42. K. Santhanam and Ramakant Dwivedi(eds.), *India and Central Asia Advancing the Common Interest,* New Delhi, 2004, pp. 3-9;*The Hindu,* 2/2/2002

43. *The Times of India*, Patna, 25, 6, 2003
44. *Press Release in Russian*, Dushanbe, 17 November 2003
45. Gulshan Luthra, "India extends strategic reach with Tajikistan base", *Indo-Asian News Service*,November14, 2003
46. *Indo-Iranica,* Toshkent, 2002, p. 22
47. *The Hindu,23/6/2003*
48. *The Hindu,24/6/2003*
49. *The Hindu,17/10/2003*

Bibliography

Primary Sources

In Russian Language

Abulgani Mirzoev, Mahmood Hasan Siddiqi and Saiyid Hisamuddin Rashidi (eds.), Mutribi's *Khatirat-i- Mutrabi*, Karanchi, 1976-77.

Biruni, *Indiya,* Tahkent, 1963.

G.G. Kotovskii, Bibliografiya Indii, Uoskva, 1965.

ICANAS—2004, *Brochure,* Moscow, 2004.

Narody Vostoka Indii-Strana I Narod, Book 2, Moscow, 1972.

P.M. Shastitko (chief editor), *Rossiiskiye Puteshestvenniki V Indii XIX-Nachalo XX V.*, Moscow, 1990.

P.M.Shastitko (chief editor), *Russko- Indiiskiye Otnosheniya v XIX v.* , Moskva, 1997.

R. G. Mukminova, *Sotsialnaya Differentsatsiya Naseleniya Gorodov Uzbekistana,* Tashkent, 1985.

Sadriddin Aini, *Sobraniye Sochinenii*, Vol.V (Bukhara), Moskva,1974.

S. D. Miliband, *Bibliograficheskii Slovar Otechestvennykh Vostokovedov*, Vols I and II , Moscow, 1995.

T. K. Bishembiev, *Tarikh-i- Shahrukhi,*Alma-Ata, 1987.

Zagorodnikova and Shastitko (chief editors), *Russko-Indiiskiye Otnoshenya 1900-1917gg.*, Moskva, 1999.

In English Language

Annual Report Of The Ministry Of External Affairs, Government Of India, New Delhi, 1992-93.

Ashoke Kumar Mukhopadhyay (ed), *India And Communism Secret Documents,* Calcutta, 1997.

Dietrich Reetz, *Hijrat : The flight of the Faithful A British file on the Exodus of Muslim Peasants from North India to Afghanistan* : 1920, Berlin, 1995.

Etherton, *In The Heart Of Asia,* London, 1925.

F. M. Bailey, *Mission to Tashkent,* London, 1946.

Information Bulletin, Issue 20, Moscow, 1994.

K. A. Antonova, "Recollection of Personal Encounters With Indians In The USSR In 1930s-1940s", *The Social Engineer,* Vol. 9, No.1, January 2000.

L. Kharyukov, *Friendship University*, Soviet Land Booklets, New Delhi, 1991.

Mahendra Pratap, *My Life Story Of Fifty five Years,* Delhi, 1974.

M. N. Roy, *Memoirs,* Bombay, 1964.

Muzaffar Ahmad, *Myself and the Communist Party of India,* Calcutta, 1970.

Purabi Roy, Sobhanlal Datta Gupta and Hari Vasudevan (eds.), Indo- Russian Relations 1917-1947, Part I 1917-1928, Calcutta, 1999.

Roy, Datta Gupta and Vasudevan (eds), *Indo-Russian Relations* 1917-47, Part II, 1929-47, Calcutta, 2000.

South Asian Languages Department, Tashkent, 1997.

Shaukat Usmani, " India and Russian Revolution III", *Mainstream,* New Delhi July 15, 1967.

Shaukat Usmani, *Historic Trips of a Revolutionary: Sojourn in the Soviet Union,* Delhi, 1977.

Secondary Sources

In Russian Language

A.E. Snesaryev, "Zheleznaya doroga v Kashmir", *Svedeniya,* Tashkent, 1990.

A.I. Vygornitskii, *Psobiye dlya izucheniya yazika industani (Urdu) i voyenny* slovar *russko-industani,* Tashkent, 1898.

Azizov, "Na Indo-Afganskoye Granitse Vosstaniye afganskikh plemen", Na *Zarubezhnom Vostoke,* Tashkent, 1933, No 3-4 pp. 119-128.

A.V. Raikov, *Probuzhdeniye Indii*, Moscow, 1968.

Baba Khojayev, *Russko-Afghanskiye Torgoviye-Ekonomicheskiye Otnosheniya Vo Vtoroi Polovine XVIII – Nachale XXv.*, Tashkent, 1965.

B. Abidov, "Contribution of Institute of Oriental Studies of Uzbek Academy of Sciences to Strengthening of Indo-Uzbek Relation", *South Asia And Central Asia*, Tashkent,1997, p.31.

Baikova, "Iz istorii karavannoi torgovli mezhdu Srednei Azii I Severnoi Indii v XIXv." in *Vzamootnosheniya narodov Srednei Azii i sopredelnikh stran Vostoka v XVIII—nachal XX v.*, pp. 163-194.

B.A.Litviskii "Bobojon Gafurovich Gafurov—Osnovopolozhnik Tajikskoi Istoriicheskoi Naukoi," in *V Masshtabe* Veka, Moskva, 1999.

B. I. Iskandrov, *Srednyaya Aziya I Indiya,* Dushanbe, 1993.

B.T.Abidov and A.R.Sahibaev, "India V Trudakh Uchenykh Instituta Vostokovedeniya Akademii Nauk Uzbekistana" (cyclostyled copy).

Byuletin presy Sred Vostoka, Tashkent, 1928.

D. Ferestanov, "Britanskay voennay ekspaditsiya v polosy nezabisimikh plemen (iyul-sentyambr), 1933", *Na Zarubezhnom Vostoke.* Tashkent, 1933.

G. G. Kotovskii, "Bobojan Gafurovich Gafurov—Glava Sovetskogo Vostokovedeniya" in V Masshtabe Veka, Moscow, 1999.

G.L. Dmitriyev, *Iz Istorii Sredneaziatsko-Indiiskikh Otnoshenii Vtoroi Poloviny XIX-Nachala XX V. (Indiiskiye Vykhodtsy V Srednei Azii), Avtoreferat,* Tashkent, 1965.

G.L. Dmitriyev, "Iz Istorii Indiiskikh Kolonii V Srednei Azii" in D. A. Olderogge (chief Editor), Strany I Narody Vostoka Indii-Strana I Narod, Book 2, Moscow, 1972.

G.K.Shirokov, "B.G.Gafurov I Vostokovedeniye" in M.C.Lebedev (Compiler), *V Masshtabe Veka,* Moscow, 1999.

Ibid., "Pogranichniye zhelezniye dorogi v. Indii", *Svedeniya,* Tashkent, 1898.

Ibid., "Zheleznodorozhnaya set v Indii i vopros o soedinonii yee s proyektiruyemymi zheleznymi dorogami v kitaye", *Svedeniya,* Tashkent, 1899.

Ibid., "Anglo-Ruskiye otnosheniya na severo-zapadnoy grantise Indii", *Svedeniya,* Tashkent 1898.

Ibid., "Chitralskii vopros", *Svedeniya,* Tashkent, 1898.

Ibid., " Belujistan I svyazanniye s nim voprosy", *Svedeniya,* Tashkent, 1899. "Indiya Rabochiye dvizheniye: Revolutsnoye Krestiansoye, dvizheniye", *Na Zarubezhnom Vostoke,* Tashkent, 1932.

Ibid., Mssiya Gidermaier-Gentiga v Afghanistane (1915-16) *Kratkiye Soobsheniya Instituta Vostokovedeniya, AN, SSR, Moskva, 1960, pp. 18-26.*

Ibid., "Arrgarnaya programma Induskogo natsionalnogo kongresa", *Na Zarubezhnom Vostoke,* Tashkent, 1939, No.2, pp. 1-11.

Ibid., *Industanii-Russkii Slovar*, St. Petersberg, 1902.

Ibid., "Torgoviye shnosheniya Indii s Persiyei", *Svedeniya,* Tashkent, 1904.

Ibid., "Musulmane v Indii", *Svedeniya,* 1906, Vyp.83, No.10 pp. 17-23.

Ibid., "Indiskiye Musulmane i evropeiskaya kultura", *Svedeniya.*

Il'ias Nizamutdinov, *Iz istorii Sredneaziatsko-indiiiskikh otnoshenii (*IX-XVIII vv.), Tashkent, 1969.

I.M.Oranskii, "K Etnografii Indiyazychnoi Gruppy Parya", in *Strany I Narody Vostoka Indii—Strana I Narod,*pp.219-33.

I.M.Reisner (Reusner), "Polozheniye rabochego klassa I rabochiyeedvizheniye", *Na Zarubekhnom Vostoke,* Tashkent,1934, No.2, pp. 91-101.

Indo-Iranica, Tashkent, 2002, Contains summaries of articles in Russian Uzbek and English presented at an International Symposium on "Central Asia and South Asia: History and Modernity" held at Tashkent from 27th November to 1st December 2000 at the Tashkent State Institute of Oriental Studies.

I.P., Yagello, *Prakticheskay grammatika yazyika industani (urdu),* Taskent, 1902.

Iz Istorii progressivnom obshchestvennoi I filosofiskoi mysli v Indii, Tashkent, 1976.

Kashkin K., "Vosstaniye v Alware", *Na Zarubezhnom Vostaoke,* Tashkent, 1933.

Kasymov, *Maisura za Nezavimost v Kontse XVIII v.,* Tashkent, 1964.

K.N.Warikoo, *Central Asia and Kashmir,* New Delhi, 1989.

Kutina and Hasimov, *Deytelnost Indiiskogo Natsionalnogo*

Kongressa I Obshchestvennogo Organizatsii Indii Kontse XIX I Nachalo XXV, Tashkent, 1988.

Losyev, "Togovlya c Zapadnym Tibetim (Industansko-tibetskii put)" *Svedeniya* Tashkent, 1906, vyp. 81, No. 8.

Losyev, "Miting magometan v Bombye", *Svedeniya,* 1906, Vyp. 1, No. 8, pp. 32-33.

L.I.Miroshnikov, "Akademik B.G.Gafurov I Izucheniye Middle And Central Asia" in *V Masshtabe* Veka, Moskva, 1999.

Maliev, *Hinduston Angliyaning astindah* (in Uzbek Language), Tashkent, 1920.

M. B. Baratov, *Leninism and Social Thought in India(* in Uzbek Language), Tashkent, 1973.

M.S. Asimov, "Tsentralnaya Aziya v Drevnosti: Problemy Istorii I Kultury", in *Budushchyeye Nauki,* Moscow, 1983, pp. 254-269.

M. Grulev, "Anglo-Russkiye otnosheniya na severo-zapadnoy grantise Indii", *Svedeniy kasayushiyesya stran sopredelnikh s Turkestan. Voyein.Okrugom* (hereafter cited as *Svedeniya)* , Tashkent 1898.

M. M. Khairullaev,P.G.Bulgakov,U. M. Ariper and I.M.Khasimov (eds), *Narodov Srednei Azii I Indii,*Tashkent, 1986.

M. M. Kutina, *Ekonomcheskiye Svyazi Uzbekistana c Indiyei,* Taskent, 1984.

M.P. Pavlovich ((Weltman), *India V Borbe Za Nezavisimost,* Moscow, 1925.

Muzaffar Olimov, *Ocherki Istorii Sinda V XVII-Nachale XIX V.,* Moscow, 1993.

Ocherki istorii peredvoi obshchestvenno-filosofiskoi mysli narodovZarubezhnogo Vostoka, Tashkent, 1971.

P. N. Rasul-zade, *Is Istorii Srdne-Aziatsko-Indiskikh Svyazei Vtoroi Poloviny XIX-nachala XX Veka,* Tashkent, 1968.

Stavisky, *Sudba Buddisma V Srednei Azii*, Moscow, 1998.

South Asia And Central Asia: The Past And The Present, Tashkent, 1997 (contains summaries of papers in Uzbek, Russian and English languages presented in the Conference dedicated to 50th Anniversary of South Asian Languages Department, Tashkent).

T. Scott, " Vosstaniye v Kashmire", trans, from English by D.

Ferestanov, *Byul. Zarubezhnoy Voeyn-presy no Vostoky,* Tashkent, 1933, No.1, pp. 1-13.

Vzamootnosheniya narodov Srednei Azii I sopredelnikh stran Vostoka v XVIII—nachal XXv., Tashkent, 1963.

In English Language

A. Rajabov and V. Mirzoeva (editor-in-chiefs), *Bobojan Gafurov, Investigator Of History And Culture Of Peoples From Central Asia,* Dushanbe, 1999. The book contains articles in Russian and Persian languages with summaries in English.

A.N.Shamatov, "South Asian Studies In Uzbekistan", *Journal Of Historical Studies*, Patna University, No.4, December 1998

Aruna Haldar, "Lonely, Majestic Sojourner," *The Times Of India,* Patna, 12 July 1993

Ata Khurseed, "Dictionaries & Grammar Books Of Uzbek (Chugtai-Turkish) Language & Other Manuscripts Preserved In Maulana Azad Library, Aligarh," *Historical and Cultural Links,* pp. 397-40

B. B. Reznikov, "The Comintern's Oriental Policy" in R. A. Ulyanvosky(ed.), *The Comintern and the East A Ciritique of the Critique*, Moscow, 1978

C. S. Samra, *India and Anglo-Soviet Relations, 1917-1947,* Bombay, 1959

Claude Markovits, *The Global World Of Indian Merchants 1750-1947 Traders of Sind from Bukhara to Panama,* Cambridge University Press,Cambridge (U.K.),2000

Contemporary Central Asia, Vol III, No.1, 1999

Devendra Kaushik, *India And Central Asia In Modern Times*,New Delhi, 1985,

Etherton, *In The Heart Of Asia,* London, 1925

G.L.Dmitriev (Dmitriyev), *The Indian Revolutionaries in Central Asia,* Gurgaon, 2002

G.L.Dmitriyev, "From the History of Indian Colony in Central Asia" in Surendra Gopal (ed), *India and Central Asia,* Delhi, 2001, pp. 76-98

Gafurov,B., "Bahr al-Asrar II", *Journal of the Pakistan Historical Society*,14/2 (1966)

Gulshan Luthra, "India extends strategic reach with Tajikistan base", *Indo-Asian News Service*,November14, 2003

H.N.Pandit, *Netaji Subhas Chandra Bose From Kabul to Battle of Imphal,* Sterling Publishers Private Limited, Delhi, n.d.

Historical and Cultural Links between India & Uzbekistan, Khuda Bakhsh International Seminar, 1993, Patna, 1996

Ibid., "India and Central Asia : Political Contacts from Colonial Period to Aftermath of the Socialist Revolution" in Surendra Gopal(ed), *India and Central Asia,* Delhi, 2001, pp. 99-138

Ibid., "Indian Traders in Uzbekistan in the Eighteenth Century," in Surendra Gopal (ed.), *India and Central Asia, pp. 19-43*

Journal of The Royal Central Asian Society, 1933

Journal of The Royal Central Asian Society, 1936

K. N. Warikoo, *Central Asia and Kashmir,* New Delhi, 1989

K. Santhanam and Ramakant Dwivedi(eds.), *Indian and Central Asia Advancing the Common Interest,* New Delhi, 2004, pp. 3-9.

L.Kharyukov, *Friendship University*, Sovietland Booklets, New Delhi, 1991

M. A. Persists, *Revolutionaries of India in Soviet Russia,* Moscow, 1973

M. Blagonravova, *The Youth of the USSR and India,* Novosti Press Agency publishing House, Moscow, 1974 "Central Asia in Antiquity: Problems of History and Culture", in *Budushchyeye Nauki* , Moscow, 1983.

M.A. Persists, "Eastern Internationalists in Russia And Some Questions of the National Liberation Movement (1918-July 1920)" in Ulyanovsky (ed.), *The Comintern and the East* (Moscow, 1979)

M.S. Asimov and C.E. Bosworth (eds) *History of Civilizations of Central Asia,* Volume IV, Part One, First Indian Edition, Delhi, 1999

Panchanan Saha, *Shapurji Saklatvala,* New Delhi, 1970

Polinova,*Realism in Contemporary Indian Novels*, Tashkent, 1984.

Richard C. Foltz, *Mughal India And Central Asia,* Oxford University Press, Karachi,1998

S. M. Mehdi, *The Story behind 'Moscow-Tashkent Conspiracy Case ?,Delhi, 1967*

Scott C. Levi, *The Indian Diaspora in Central Asia and its Trade 1550-1900*, Leiden, 2002

Shail Mayaram, "Komal Kothari rooted in oral tradition", *The Hindu,* 20 June 2004.

Stephen Dale, *The Garden Of The Eight Paradises,* Brill, Leiden, 2004

Surendra Gopal (ed) *India and Central Asia Cultural, Economic and Political Links* ,Delhi, 2001

Surendra Gopal "Comintern and the Indian Communist Party: The Early Year", *Socialist Perspective*, Vol. 28 No. 1-2, June – September, 2000, pp. 67-75

Surendra Gopal, "The Travelogue Of A Russian Officer In India" in *Proceedings*, Indian Historical Records Commission, Vol. XLIII, Lucknow Session, 1975

Surendra Gopal, *Indian Freedom-Fighters In Tashkent:1917-1922 Contesting Ideologies: Nationalism, Pan Islamism and Marxism*, Kolkata, 2002

Surendra Gopal, "India and Soviet Central Asia in Pre-Independence Days', *Dialogue,* Vol. 3 No.4, April-June 2002

T.R. Sareen, *British Intervention In Central Asia and Trans-Caucasia,* New Delhi, 1989

The Central Asian Quarterly, Vol.3 No.4,1996

Zafar Imam, "The Al-Beruni Library- A Live Symbol Of Indo-Uzbek Cross Culture" in *Historical and Cultural Links*, pp. 426-31.

Sources in Hindi, Urdu and Bengali Languages

Aloke Raj, *Uzbekistan Gantantra, Kamyabi Ka Safanama,* Patna, 2001, pp.8-9.

Chinmoy Sehanavis, *RusBiplab Pravasi Bhartiya Biplabi, (Bengali),* Calcutta, 1973.

Dmitry Volsky, *The Developments In The Indian Subcontinent And The Soviet Union* (in Hindi), Delhi, 1972.

Rahul Sankrityayan, *Meri Jeevan Yatra* (in Hindi) ,Volume II,

Allahabad, 1950.
Rahul Sankrityayan, *Madhya Asiya ka Itihas* (in Hindi) ,Part I, Patna, 1956.
Zafar Hassan, *Ap Beeti*, (in Urdu),Lahore, 1955.

Newspapers

The Asian Age, 9 / 2/ 2001.
The Central Asian Quarterly Vol. 3, No. 4,1996.
The Hindu, 19/ 7 / 1954.
The Hindu, 23 / 11 /1995.
The Hindu, 17/7/2000.
The Hindu, 12/8/2000.
The Hindu, Nov. 2000.
The Hindu, 11/9/2000.
The Hindu, 5 / 1 / 2001.
The Hindu 6/1/2001.
The Hindu, 29/4/2001.
The Hindu, 11/5/2001.
The Hindu , 26/5/2001.
The Hindu, 15/6/2001.
The Hindu, 11/7/2001.
The Hindu, 30 / 8 /2001.
The Hindu, 31/8/2001.
The Hindu, 6/9/2001.
The Hindu, 26/10/2001.
The Hindu, 2/2/2002.
The Hindu, 21/10/2002.
The Hindu, 7/11/2002.
The Hindu, 25/12/2002.
The Hindu, 3 / 2/ 2003.
The Hindu, 27/1/2003.
The Hindu, 11/6/2003.
The Hindu, 23/6/2003.
The Hindu, 24/6/2003.
The Hindu, 17/10/2003.
Press Release in Russian, Dushanbe, 17 November 2003.
The Times of India, 15/2/2001.
The Times of India, 19/2/1998.

The Times of India, Patna, 25/6/2003.
The Times of India, 23/9/2000.

Newspapers (Consulted)

Indo-Asian News Service
The Asian Age
The Hindu
The Times of India

Journals (Consulted)

Contemporary Central Asia
Information Bulletin
The Central Asian Quarterly

Index